Contents

Cover: Fossiled Devonian fish from Scotland, with items from the *Game of life*.

Inside & back cover: The Wenlock Limestone, a Silurian reef deposit from the Welsh borders, full of shells and coral debris.

What are fossils?

Everyone is familiar with the stunning fossils held in museums. They are beautiful and delicate reminders of the age of the Earth and of the diversity of life. Most of the fossils that we ourselves might find on beaches or in quarries are imperfect and damaged by their time in the rocks; but these common fossils contain vital information, for they are our direct evidence for the past life of our planet, Earth.

A bone or a shell, a footprint or a feeding trace, are the clues left by animals and plants from which we are able to reconstruct their lives. These clues can be used to assess the environments in which fossils lived. A fossil might contain information about the temperature of the sea in which the living organism swam, or demonstrate the existence of old and now vanished oceans. Fossils allow the slow movements of continents to be traced from past to present. By studying their shape and the patterns of their evolution, fossils enable us to build up a picture of the history of life on our planet and the great evolutionary forces which have changed the face of our world.

The record of the past left by fossils is an incomplete one. Fossilisation is rare: most animals and plants are eaten at, or after, death, and their chemical constituents recycled. Few find their way into a quiet area where sediment is accumulating. Even fewer survive the violent upheavals of our active planet. Only a tiny fraction of the fossils which do form are found and studied by palaeontologists.

I study the fossils of a group of marine animals which lived around 450 million years ago. In Welsh quarries and on Scottish hillsides these graptolites (as they are called) are abundant (1). This group changed shape rapidly as it evolved, and these changes can be likened to a clock

1 Graptolites from southern Scotland. *Diplograptus cf. modestus* is Ordovician in age and about 2 cm long.

2 The fossil of an ammonite, *Promicroceras planicosta*.

3 Fossils are occasionally found articulated. *Eryon arctiformis* is found in the Solnhofen Limestone in Bavaria.

Investigating the past history of the Earth is no empty study, carried out in museums and universities for the benefit of a few and taught to students who might prefer to be elsewhere. It is a vital part of the process of understanding our world. It is also one of our best hopes of learning to predict the future and the likely effects of global warming or of ozone holes. At times in the past the Earth was ozone free, at other times it was a greenhouse world. By studying the response of organisms to such states, we can estimate how they will affect the future and how they will effect us.

which dates the rocks in which they lie. A block of shale 420 million years old can be dated by graptolites to the nearest 100 000 years, an extraordinary precision which is unmatched by any other technique. At the same time, in the shape-changing of my graptolites is a narrative of change and a measure of evolutionary theory, such as Darwin's. These small and unassuming fossils also show that a large ocean, possibly 1500 km wide, separated England and Scotland at the time when they lived. They thus chart the movement of continents through the eons.

4 A trace fossil — the temporary resting place of a brittle starfish from the Triassic rocks of Italy.

How fossils form

Of the millions of organisms which die each day, only a tiny fraction will be fossilised. There are two steps in this process: first, the organism must be buried and entombed in rock; second, compression and chemical change are needed to produce fossils.

After death, most organisms are eaten, or they decay and their constituents are recycled. Only exceptional circumstances cause an organism to be buried intact, or with all of the hard elements of the skeleton together (5).

Each of the three fossils on this page give useful insights into the processes which occur during preservation. The fern (1), ammonite (2) and fish (3) have undergone an unusual sequence of events which have led them to be fossilised. While the fish and the ammonite were dead before this sequence of events began, the fern is only a frond, and the tree on which it grew might well have survived its loss.

All three specimens escaped scavenging, which can scatter or destroy remains, and

1 *Archaeopteris hibernicus*, a Devonian tree fern preserved as a flattened carbon film

all three were buried before they had time to decay. This implies unusually rapid burial for the fish (as they normally decay quickly) and for the tree fern. However, the ammonite must have been buried more slowly as its soft tissue is gone. In general, organisms with a one-piece, durable skeleton have the best chance of becoming fossilised as their hard parts survive the process of decay. Obviously, fossils can only form where sediment is accumulating, in order for burial to occur at all.

After an organism is buried, the second stage begins — that of transforming it into a fossil. Physical stresses have an effect — most plant fossils are preserved as flattened impressions because the originals have been crushed by the weight of rock above them (1). Most organisms which are preserved in shales and clays are crushed by the extreme compaction of these rocks after burial. Deformation of rocks in which fossils lie can distort them as the sediment grains are strained and recrystallised (4).

Chemical changes have a profound effect on fossilisation.

3 *Naso rectifrons*, an Eocene fish (about 6 cm long) preserved intact but flattened.

2 *Oxynoticeras lymense*, a Jurassic ammonite with a shell replaced by pyrite.

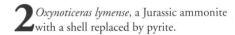

4 Trilobites *(Angelina sedgwickii)* distorted after burial.

The aragonite of an ammonite shell can be dissolved and replaced by sediment or by another mineral such as pyrite (fool's gold) (2). Iridescent aragonite is unstable, and over millions of years will convert to a stable equivalent, calcite. Organic fossils such as leaves are frequently replaced by clays or complex mineral assemblages (1).

In general then, the organisms with the greatest fossilisation potential are those with a hard, external skeleton, small size and a lifestyle which involves living in an area where sediment is accumulating. Poor chances of fossilisation result from being large, having an articulated or internal skeleton, having no skeleton at all, or living in an area where rocks are being eroded rather than deposited. In practice, most fossils are invertebrates (animals without backbones) which live or lived in shallow seas. Other environments are much more poorly represented in the fossil record.

5 Two echinoderms preserved in different settings. *Acrosalenia hemicidaroides* (left) has begun to decay before burial and is falling apart. *Ophiurella speciosa* (above) was buried as it died and is perfectly preserved.

5

Exceptional fossils

Any fossil represents a rare event, when a dead organism was buried or preserved before it could be scavenged and destroyed. However, some fossil localities have a special interest to palaeontologists, either because of the quality, or sheer quantity of the fossils preserved there. These abnormal deposits are called fossil- *lagerstätten*, from a German quarrying term, meaning a rock with constituents of economic interest.

Storms on the sea bed can concentrate fossils into great numbers which are preserved on certain planes in the rocks (5). These fossil concentrations are spectacular, and also important because they record the environment in which the animals lived and the physical and chemical conditions in which their skeletons were deposited. Hard parts lying on the sea bed will normally be attacked by scavengers, be abraded by physical movements and break down chemically. Some types of shell are more susceptible to each of these processes than others. Ammonites, for example, had shells composed of a relatively unstable form of calcium carbonate, called aragonite, which was particularly prone to chemical decay by sea water. The presence of abundant ammonites in a concentration *lagerstätte* shows that the shells were buried quickly, which prevented them from corroding, but were then concentrated by a later storm which exhumed them from their individual burial sites to be transported and deposited together, like cockles on a modern beach.

Rarer than diamond mines, there are localities where fossils are preserved in

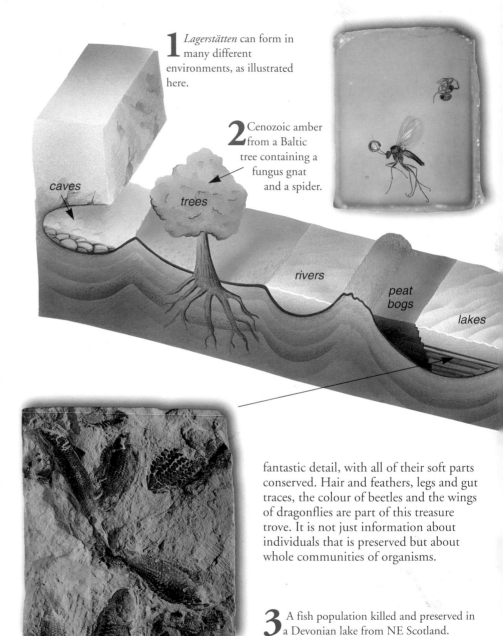

1 *Lagerstätten* can form in many different environments, as illustrated here.

2 Cenozoic amber from a Baltic tree containing a fungus gnat and a spider.

caves

trees

rivers

peat bogs

lakes

fantastic detail, with all of their soft parts conserved. Hair and feathers, legs and gut traces, the colour of beetles and the wings of dragonflies are part of this treasure trove. It is not just information about individuals that is preserved but about whole communities of organisms.

3 A fish population killed and preserved in a Devonian lake from NE Scotland.

Exceptional fossils

4 *Limulus*, the horseshoe crab, preserved in the lagoonal sediments of the Jurassic Solnhofen Limestone of Bavaria.

5 A mass of broken stems of sea lilies (crinoids), from a Carboniferous reef in the Pennines.

A characteristic set of conditions is needed for organisms to be preserved intact. The most important of these seems to be a lack of oxygen. In some environments, especially in quiet seas, oxygen becomes depleted in the muds of the sea floor and decay is slowed. One problem is that very few organisms, or potential fossils, thrive in low oxygen concentrations. Most *lagerstätten* fossils were brought into the environment where they were preserved after, or as, they died. Sometimes the sediment trapping the fossils was brought into the area at the same time as the organisms. Sometimes this sediment blanketed the area later. However, only areas of net sedimentation can become a *lagerstätte*.

shallow seas

reefs

deep seas

Predators and prey are both preserved along with scavengers, parasites and bacteria. The reasons for the preserving of such wonderful detail are varied, from freezing in ice to rapid death in an oversalty lagoon.

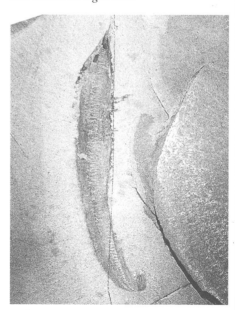

6 One of our oldest relatives, the chordate, *Pikaia*, from the deep water, middle Cambrian, Burgess Shale of Canada.

Evolution

Fossils show that organisms have changed their shape and life habits throughout geological time. This is evolution — the capacity of life forms to change in response to stress, and to maintain that change through the generations. Any fossiliferous area records this, literally in stone, without any room for doubt. Evolution is a demonstrable fact not open to dispute. Much more controversial are the means by which evolution occurs and the forces which drive it. Theories have been debated by biologists for centuries and the study of fossils plays a key role in arbitrating between the likelihood of different ideas.

In 1859, Charles Darwin (1), an innovative geologist as well as a great biologist, published his book *On the Origin of Species by Natural Selection*. In it, he proposed that a simple natural force causes evolution. It was a Victorian idea which fitted well with the social environment of the day and it is often paraphrased as 'survival of the fittest'. Darwin suggested that any population of organisms has the potential to breed more individuals than the environment can support. He noted that in any group there are differences between individuals. He proposed that those individuals who, by chance, had a slight advantage over their neighbours would be more likely to survive long enough to breed successfully. The characteristics of the successful would be more common in the next generation so that over time the characteristics of the whole population would change.

Palaeontologists accept this idea because there is convincing evidence for gradual change within the fossil record. A perfect example was investigated in Wales by a lecturer at the Open University, Dr Peter Sheldon. He examined thousands of trilobites, including *Ogygiocarella* and *Cnemidopyge*, and was able to chart their slow changes in shape and size over about three million years (2).

Intriguingly, though, such ideal examples are rare in the fossil record. Fossiliferous sections commonly show sudden jumps in shape occurring with no gradual build up. These jumps are followed by long periods of time when no change can be measured. For many people, an adequate explanation is found in the incompleteness of fossil preservation: after all, a million years of deep sea ooze can be washed away during a single storm.

However, over the last 25 years another theory has emerged to explain this

1 Charles Darwin.

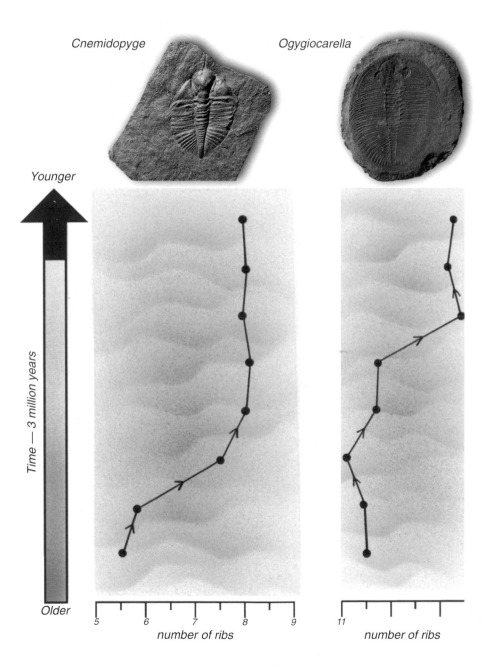

Cnemidopyge

Ogygiocarella

Younger

Time — 3 million years

Older

number of ribs

number of ribs

punctuated pattern. Professors Eldridge and Gould, then at the University of Chicago, have caused a revolution in the interpretation of the fossil record with their theory of punctuated equilibrium. They suggest that most populations have a stable relationship with the environment and any slight changes in the frequency of a particular character are averaged out over generations. However, small, isolated populations, and those under great environmental stress, change very rapidly. The characters of a few individuals can have a great effect on the characters of a subsequent generation. A rapidly evolving, isolated group may then become well adapted to a range of environments and spread out over a larger area. In most of the fossil record, only their appearance through migration would be recorded and evolution would appear to occur in sudden jumps. This is still a Darwinian view of selection, but modified by subsequent observations.

Fossils can thus give evidence which supports or contradicts differing theories of evolution. Their study can demonstrate how fast evolution occurs and how much change is possible. Fossils also record the random path of evolution which led to the origin of man. However, in its incompleteness, the fossil record is one of the most tantalising of witnesses.

2 The number of ribs on two species of trilobite changed gradually over about 3 million years, suggesting that evolution acts constantly rather than in short bursts.

Dating the Earth

1 *Oxynoticeras oxynotum,* an ammonite used to date rocks of lower Jurassic age.

How old are the White Cliffs of Dover, or the rocks of the Lake District? How ancient are the rocks below London? One answer comes from fossils which were trapped in these sediments as they formed. Sedimentary rocks are those which were laid down on the surface of the Earth, perhaps in a swampy lagoon or beneath the sea. Sealed, in the fossils they contain, is a record of both the environments of their formation and their age. By deducing the ages of different rocks, and the environments in which they were formed, a history of the British Isles can be built up. One of the primary uses of fossils is in dating rocks, a study known as *biostratigraphy*.

Biostratigraphy is possible because the organisms which formed fossils evolved, changing shape with time. Some of these shape changes were recorded in their preserved hard parts and act as a clock to measure the geological past. The rates of evolution were faster for some groups of organisms than for others. Rapidly evolving groups make exceptionally good fossil clocks. Ammonites (1) are an excellent example, changing their shape and the ornamentation of their whorls very rapidly and allowing the relative dating of rocks with unparalleled precision. Rare organisms which seem not to have evolved at all, like the horseshoe crab (2), cannot be used for dating rocks.

As the fossil record is imperfect, most rock sections contain only a sample of the fossils of their time. Erosion frequently removes sediments from an area, and with them the record of that slice of time. Rocks deposited in different environments but at the same time contain organisms suited to particular conditions, and there may be no overlap between them. These features of the rocks present problems of correlation, a problem of comparing the ages of different sections of sediment. However, the great strength of the rock record for allowing dating is a simple phenomena known as the *Law of Superimposition* (3). This is a straightforward idea, that a rock layer must be younger than the layer below it and older than the layer above it. Once this was deduced, dating of the rocks by fossils could proceed rapidly.

Some fossils provide better data than others to help us overcome these problems. Rapidly evolving organisms are ideal, but they must have had hard parts which were readily preserved as fossils and which recorded their evolution. Common fossils are much more useful than rare ones, and the incredibly abundant microfossils are amongst the most powerful tools for biostratigraphy. Finally, a widespread distribution is needed, which requires the organism to have been tolerant of many different environments and able to spread over large distances. The best lifestyle for dating fossils is a planktic one. Planktic organisms are abundant, live above many different sea beds and float throughout their lives across the world's oceans (4).

2 *Limulus,* the horseshoe crab. This Jurassic example looks exactly like living forms. Such slow evolvers are useless in dating rocks.

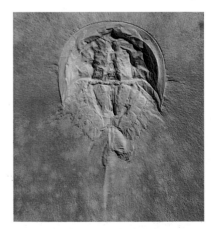

The greatest failure of fossil evidence in dating rocks is that their 'clock' lacks a 'dial'. Fossils can show if one rock is older or younger than another, but not by how much. Calibration of the fossil record must be done using the rate of decay of elements in the rocks themselves. It is a laborious and expensive process to date rocks using the decay of unstable atoms, but one that gives an absolute time scale as each element decays at a fixed and known rate. This calibration of fossils through comparison with unstable isotopes, as they are known, is a recent phenomenon. Before it became possible, relative dating was the only method, and rock units were given names based on the area where they were well exposed or first studied.

The list of geological periods is familiar to many schoolchildren and is still of great value today. It is simpler to think of a fossil or a rock being of Devonian age than to refer to it as being between 417–354 million years old, especially as these 'absolute' ages are only estimates which change with great frequency.

3 *The Law of Superimposition* — layers of rocks reveal their relative ages as the lower layers must be older. Absolute dates can be added by correlation with rocks dated by radioactive isotopes.

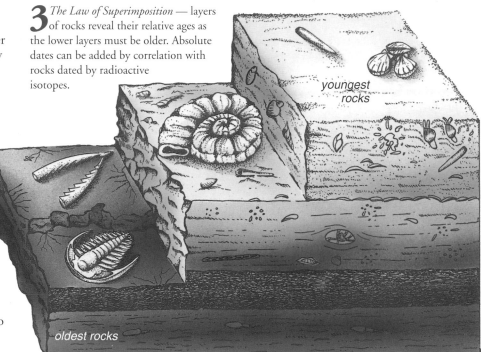

youngest rocks

oldest rocks

4 Graptolites like *Didymograptus* make perfect fossils for dating rocks because of their abundance, rapid evolution and planktic lifestyle.

5 Trilobites like *Angelina sedgwickii* are useful fossils for dating rocks, but were often restricted to particular environments.

Travelling continents

In 1914, Alfred Wegener published a book entitled *The origin of continents and oceans*, in which he put forward the theory that continents drift slowly across the globe. He showed that the fit of South America and Africa was like two pieces of a jigsaw and suggested that they had once been joined together. One of his most powerful pieces of evidence was from fossils. A widespread flora dominated by *Glossopteris* trees (1) was common to both continents in the Permian period, as was a freshwater Jurassic dinosaur which could not possibly have crossed an ocean had the Atlantic been present during its migrations.

Since the 1960s, this theory of continental drift has been given new impetus by the theory of plate tectonics. We now know that the Earth's crust is made up of a series of separate plates which jostle together in response to the movement of currents in the mantle below. Continents separate and oceans form where plates are pulled apart. They collide as the crust below an ocean is destroyed where plates meet. The flora and fauna of the past record these

2 By the Devonian, freshwater fish were common on both sides of the old Iapetus Ocean,

continental movements as times of independent evolution and times of faunal mixing.

Five hundred million years ago, an ocean separated Scotland from England. Along the line of the future Solway Firth ran a long and fairly narrow ocean which formed around the beginning of the Cambrian and was destroyed throughout the latter half of the Silurian. We can reconstruct the size and duration of this *Iapetus* ocean by its effects on the

marine organisms which lived in it. During early Ordovician times when the ocean was at its widest, the trilobites and brachiopods from each side were profoundly different from one another. As the ocean closed, faunas on each side became more similar, until, in the Silurian and Devonian, freshwater fish and small arthropods called ostracodes became common to both sides, indicating a land connection between Scotland and England (2).

The Iapetus Ocean was one of many which separated the continents of the Lower Palaeozoic, but which have completely disappeared today. Planktic organisms left fossil 'rims' around these ancient continental margins. During the Ordovician period, the most common

1 *Glossopteris.*

Modern day

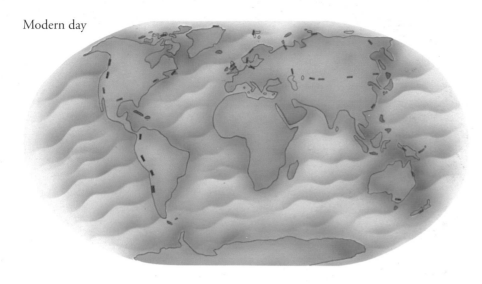

Ordovician

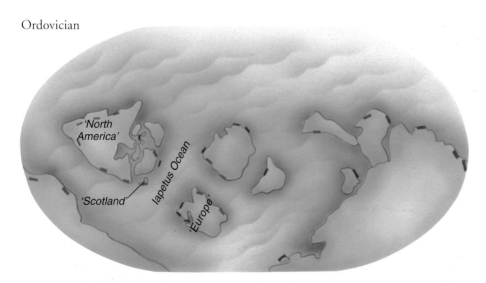

3 The modern distribution of planktic organisms holds a key to reconstructing old oceans. Deep water *Isograptus* (dashes) appears today to have a random distribution until it is displayed on the ancient pattern of continents.

group of large planktic organisms were graptolites, which are now extinct. Forms such as *Isograptus* lived in deep water, with a group of smaller species characterised by *Didymograptus* living in shallower areas. The distribution of offshore *Isograptus* looks chaotic on a modern map, but falls into sensible focus when it is plotted on a palaeogeographic map of the time (3).

Land organisms are sensitive recorders of the break-up and collision of continents. The break-up of the supercontinent, Pangaea, during the Mesozoic separated South America and Australasia from the other land masses, and had a profound effect on the evolution of mammals in those areas.

While placental mammals elsewhere carry their young in a womb, marsupials evolved in these newly separated continents and carry their young in pouches for most of the gestation period. Kangaroos and wallabies are living evidence of continental drift.

The rarity of large marsupials in South America today records a continental collision. Around six million years ago, a chain of volcanic islands began to appear in the narrowing strait between North and South America. These gradually coalesced to form the Panama isthmus around three million years ago. Migration of marsupial mammals to the north and placentals into the south has continued since then, but many of the large southern marsupials, such as the giant ground sloth, have become extinct.

Past environments

The Earth's climate controls the distribution of plants and animals in the modern world. Palm trees and reefs are indicators of warm climates, polar bears of extreme cold. The diversity of species is also climatically controlled: for example, there are more than 500 species of bivalve shellfish in some parts of the tropics, but this falls to under 100 towards the poles. In the same way, the ancient organisms preserved as fossils give a record of the climate of the world in which they lived. Scientists can use this record, along with their global distribution, to determine the patterns of climate change on our planet over the last 550 million years.

2 Modern temperate leaves.

The process of measuring ancient climatic change is easiest in the relatively recent past, when many modern species were present. Comparing the distribution of the modern form with the geography of its fossils can show if the climate has changed. The pollen and spores of many cold climate or tundra plants were left across Britain during the last two million years, and record the ebb and flow of the last Ice Age in great detail.

The general shape of some plants can give important information about ancient climates. The leaves of modern tropical plants tend to be large, with entire margins and elongated tips which allow water to

1 Modern tropical leaves.

3 An *Aralia* leaf from Bournemouth. This Eocene plant indicates warm climates; its modern relatives include ginseng.

4 Fossil tree trunk from Antarctica.

flow off the leaf surface. They often have a waxy coating to discourage predators and minimise water loss (1). On the other hand, temperate leaves tend to be smaller and have a thinner cuticle. They lack drip-tips and often have a complicated, or non-entire, shape (2). The appearance of tropical leaves in the Eocene rocks of the London area shows that England enjoyed a warm, wet climate at this time (3).

Dramatic indicators of past climates, radically different from our own, are the fossilised tree trunks found today near both the North and South Poles. Forests grew there at many times in the past including the Permian, Cretaceous and early Cenozoic (4). Trees today cannot survive close to the poles because of the extreme cold which locks water into ice. However, at times in the past the polar regions were ice free, at least close to sea level, and trees

thrived. They were probably deciduous, losing their leaves in the six dark months of winter, and had a conical shape to minimise their mutual shading in low angle sunlight.

These polar forests highlight one of the main uses of fossils as indicators of global climate change. They show times in the past when the earth was generally warmer than at present, and times of glaciation when the Earth was similar to today. In this way fossil studies are extremely relevant in the light of our modern fears over the effects of greenhouse gases and the ecological threats from global warming.

Reefs are another excellent climatic indicator and are found throughout the whole of the Phanerozoic, from the Cambrian to the present day. Different organisms have built reefs at different times, but all have needed warm water and sunlight to extract large amounts of calcium carbonate from sea water and build it into the limestone framework of the reef. Modern reefs occur as bands on either side of the equator, and ancient reefs shared this distribution, although at

times the band was significantly wider than it is today. The drift of continents through these climatic bands is dramatically illustrated by the presence of tropical reef fossils in the Peak District and Pennines (5).

5 This coral, *Lonsdaleia floriformis*, comes from the north Pennines and is part of the tropical reef belt which lay across Britain in the Carboniferous.

The life habits of fossils

How do we know the speed of a swimming ammonite, or the habits of a predatory trilobite? Did pterosaurs fly like ducks or hawks, and did fossil snails share the chemical weapons of their living cousins? The answers to questions like these come from the field of *palaeo-ecology* — the study of the life habits and ecological adaptations of fossils.

There are several ways to study the life habits of dead animals. The first is to look at the adaptations and strategies of close living relatives. This is known as *homology*. Some fossils lack living relatives, but there may be animals in the modern world which seem to show similar adaptations to similar environmental challenges. Comparison of unrelated groups with similar features is known as *analogy*. Sometimes it is possible to verify interpretations made about fossils by testing certain properties of their anatomy. Models of trilobites

1 A Cambrian trace fossil shows the feeding trail of a trilobite truncating a worm burrow, presumably where the trilobite found lunch!

2 *Rasenia evoluta*, a Jurassic ammonite from Lincolnshire.

and graptolites have helped to elucidate their modes of life. Finally, some fossils leave not only themselves, but traces of their behaviour to posterity. Trace fossils, like walking tracks or feeding burrows, can be enormously useful when the animal responsible for them can be identified (1).

Ammonites are some of the most common fossils from the Mesozoic period (2). Their shells are found all over the beaches and in the cliffs of southern and eastern England. They were actively swimming, predatory molluscs and they have a distant relative with a similar shape, called *Nautilus*. Ammonites and

Nautilus have been evolving separately for 400 million years, and closer living relatives of ammonites are squids and cuttlefish. However, experimental work suggests that an external shell was the most important feature in the ecology of ammonites so that comparison with *Nautilus* is valid (3).

3 *Nautilus*, a distant cousin of ammonites, being fed in a flume tank to make it swim against a current.

The life habits of fossils

A major puzzle for palaeontologists is how ammonites, which were very successful and abundant, managed to compete with the similarly abundant fish, in the Mesozoic seas. Fish were rapid swimmers, using large muscles to move their fins and tail. How fast could an ammonite swim? The answer seems to be not very fast at all. The limit is imposed by the method of propulsion shared by ammonites and *Nautilus*. Both move by expelling jets of water through siphons or tubes. The problem is that water has to be expelled from a chamber of fixed size inside the

and a modern *Nautilus* can only move at about 0.3 metres per second compared with a salmon which can move at more than 1.2 metres per second (3). Ammonites may have been twice as fast as *Nautilus*, because they were able to evolve into streamlined and ornamented shapes which reduced drag. However, they would have been much slower than even a slow fish. How did they compete? Ironically the limitations of ammonite

fish and even sharks. However, we can never know for certain, and it may be that ammonites shared a more similar lifestyle with squids and octopuses than with *Nautilus*.

The flying reptiles of the Jurassic and Cretaceous periods (4) have no living relatives with even remotely similar lifestyles. However, they do have living inhabitants of the same environment in birds and bats. Analogy between the living and extinct groups has thrown

4 A newly discovered pterosaur from the Jurassic Solnhofen limestone. The head is bent around and the wing membranes are still visible.

shell of the animal. There is a limit to the amount of water that can be stored here, and also in the rate at which it can be expelled. Molluscs breath via gills which are housed in the same cavity as the water for jet propulsion. Water has to move slowly enough for breathing to take place,

design may also have been a significant advantage. Breathing and swimming at the same time takes less energy than performing both actions separately. As a consequence, living *Nautilus* can live in oxygen-poor environments where fish are excluded. If ammonites did the same they could have happily coexisted with Jurassic

new light on the flying properties of pterosaurs. Modern flying animals have a range of flying skills and these are reflected in the shape of the wing. Some wings are long and thin, designed for efficient flight and gliding. Others are stubby and fat, energetic in flight but highly manoeverable. Birds with small wings relative to their body weight are rapid flyers but cannot soar, while larger winged birds are slower. The wings of pterosaurs are similar to those of modern seabirds and aerial predators. They would have been slow flyers for their size, capable of soaring and with a high whereas most trilobites probably sifted mud for food.

These mud-grubbing trilobites lived on or beneath the sea floor, but the streamlined predators may have spent their lives swimming in the open oceans of the world.

Cyclopygid trilobites (6) with large eyes, and streamlined *Parabarrandia* (5)

degree of manoeverability. These predictions of behaviour and lifestyle fit well with the pattern of finds of fossil pterosaurs which are mainly from shallow marine deposits.

Trilobites are almost as well known as ammonites. They were abundant in the Palaeozoic between 550 and 248 million

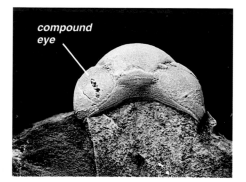

compound eye

6 A pelagic trilobite, *Pricyclopyge*, with large, forward facing eyes.

years ago. They evolved into a wide range of shapes, but are now extinct. Some trilobites, although only distantly related to one another, share a set of strange features. All are flattened and have huge eyes (6), sometimes meeting around the front. When models of these trilobites are placed in a flume tank, they prove to be extremely streamlined (5), and would have had the potential to be efficient and rapid swimmers. These trilobites were probably predators,

5 A model of a streamlined trilobite *Parabarrandia* in flowing water (top left). Compare this with the bulky, bottom-dwelling *Bumastus*, right.

also have a global distribution which supports suggestions of a life in the open sea. They may have fed on plankton and have travelled the world on the great ocean currents, settling to the bottom only in order to moult.

19

The game of life

This board game represents the evolution of life on earth: it is the 'Game of Life'.

Important elements of this 'game' are investigated in the following pages.

MASS EXTINCTION CARD

CONTINENTS COLLIDE CARD

Rules

The game of life appears to be a game of chance. Random events affect your organism's chances of survival from one time period to another. These include ice ages, continental drift and the impact of meteorites and asteroids. Biological events also affect your organism's chances of survival, from the evolution of flowers and grass to the extinction of dinosaurs. However many times you play the game of life, the result will be different each time. In fact, the whole appearance of the board may be different in alternative versions of the game.

Precambrian

The Precambrian spans all of the time between the formation of the Earth and the appearance of animals with hard parts, about 550 million years ago. It is 4000 million years long, an unimaginable stretch of time. Traces of life are sparsely scattered through Precambrian rocks. One of the vital tasks of palaeontology is to determine when life first arose on Earth and how it developed and evolved.

Sedimentary rocks form at the surface of the Earth and record the environments and atmosphere of the time. The oldest known sedimentary rocks, from Greenland, are about 3800 million years old. They record an Earth with water at the surface, and so with a surface temperature of less than 100°C. They also record the presence of oxygen bound into their chemical constituents, a product not of inorganic matter but of life. The only source for so much atmospheric oxygen is from photosynthesis, the process used by plants to derive food from sunlight, carbon dioxide and water. If plants, however primitive, were present at the time of the earliest preserved sediments, then life must have arisen even earlier (1).

The oldest known fossils are 3500 million years old, only slightly younger than the earliest sediments. They are found in Australia and South Africa and include

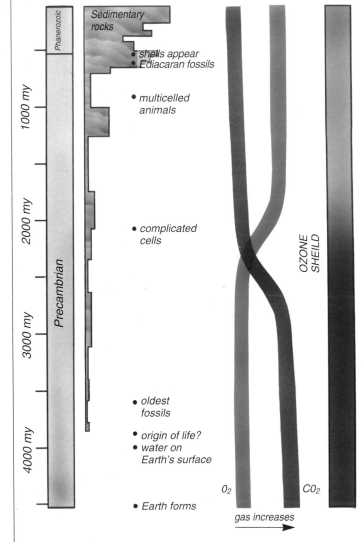

Phanerozoic

Sedimentary rocks

- shells appear
- Ediacaran fossils
- multicelled animals

1000 my

- complicated cells

2000 my

Precambrian

3000 my

- oldest fossils
- origin of life?
- water on Earth's surface

4000 my

- Earth forms

O₂   CO₂   OZONE SHIELD

gas increases →

1 Oxygen and the ozone shield (spectacularly damaged this century) are the products of life. As they built up in the atmosphere, organisms evolved with increasing complexity.

2 Stromatolites from the Aldan River in Siberia. This example is 900 million years old.

3 A multicellular green alga, 750 million years old, from Spitsbergen.

bacterial mats, known as stromatolites, and microscopic chains of cells (2). These cells were *prokaryotes*, organisms with a simple construction like modern bacteria, where the DNA is not isolated in a cell nucleus. Fossils this old are rare, but starting about 2100 million years ago the rocks have a much better record both of fossils and of the atmosphere they were altering (1). Higher levels of oxygen were introduced into the atmosphere over time, increasing the level of ultra violet protection provided by the ozone layer as well as changing the chemistry of the oceans. About 2100 million years ago the first cells with nuclei, *eukaryotes*, appeared (4). In Britain the fossil record of early life is poor, with the oldest fossils coming from Scottish rocks of the Torridon area, dated at about 900 million years old.

The astonishing things about Precambrian life are how quickly it began and how slowly it evolved subsequently. Life existed for almost 2000 million years before the first complicated cells appeared. The reasons for this are unknown, but it could be related to the amount of oxygen in the atmosphere. Oxygen builds up the ozone

layer, protecting life at the Earth's surface from harmful radiation. It is also the gas which can be most efficiently used by organisms to produce energy from food. The appearance of eukaryotes coincides with a point in time when free oxygen for respiration became ubiquitous on the Earth's surface, and with the point when an effective ozone shield could have formed. It may be that only then could the great engine of evolution got out of first gear.

The first multicelled animals *(metazoans)* were found in Namibia and then at the Ediacara Hills in South Australia: they are about 580 million years old, though multicelled plants are slightly older (3). They are now known from all over the world, including England, where they occur at Charnwood Forest in Leicestershire. They are all soft bodied

5 *Charnia*, a sea-pen like member of the Ediacaran fauna, named after Charnwood Forest where it was found. This cast is not true colour.

4 A eukaryotic cell called an acritarch. This cell is about 0.3 mm in size and 750 million years old.

and are usually poorly preserved, as moulds and casts in sandstones (5). We can identify early jellyfish with some certainty, but the nature of the other members of the fauna has caused controversy. They were certainly primitive organisms, lacking a gut and any sensory apparatus. It may be that many were unrelated to modern metazoans. Species like *Charnia* seem to have been built like quilts, or lilos, and may have extracted nutrients from their surroundings across the whole of their body surface. Even if the Ediacaran animals are related to modern groups, they seem to have no direct descendents. They became extinct at the time of a fierce ice age which occurred at the end of the Precambrian. This event may have ended the age of the Ediacarans, but it opened the history of modern multicelled life.

Cambrian

Animals with diverse shapes, sizes and functions burst into the fossil record 550 million years ago, at what is now taken to be the base of the Cambrian period. The evolution of multicelled organisms had been moving swiftly for some time before this, but the earlier animals lacked hard skeletons and so were rarely preserved as fossils. The sudden acquisition of durable, mineralized body parts increased an organism's chances of becoming fossilised. The effect for palaeontologists is as stunning and revealing as turning on an electric light in a dark room. However, the problem of how and why so many forms of life acquired skeletons at the same time is one of the biggest puzzles in palaeontology.

The geological record is divided into two by this unique event. The time prior to the appearance of common fossils is the *Precambrian*. The time afterwards, the Cambrian and younger periods, are known together as the *Phanerozoic*, the age of revealed life. In the Phanerozoic, fossils are common enough to date rocks accurately, and to show in detail how the history of life has unfolded.

The fossils which appear at the base of the Cambrian, complete with hard shells, have a wide range of body plans. Although the number of species is small, almost all of the major animal groups known today are present along with many forms which are difficult to fit into modern systems of classification. Molecular studies on modern species suggest that the earliest ancestor of modern groups must have evolved about

900 million years ago. However, the Precambrian record, which includes the soft bodied Ediacaran forms, fails to show these early ancestors of modern animals, perhaps because they were very small or lived in areas where the potential for fossilisation was low.

Mineralized skeletons are the durable and readily fossilised component of most organisms. The advantages of having a hard shell or internal skeleton are many: predators need hard teeth and claws, whilst their prey benefit from a rigid, protective

covering; muscles which are attached to a solid rod are much more efficient during movement than any of the strategies used by soft bodied forms; finally, animals with hard parts can be much larger than those without, because the body cavities and organs can be maintained in a rigid space. Moreover, some of the hard materials needed are natural waste products of animal metabolism. The surprise is not that hard parts developed, but that so many groups acquired them at the same time.

1 *Elrathia kingsi* and a small agnostid trilobite from the Cambrian rocks of North America.

2 A halkierid from Greenland, with a skeleton built from a cataphract arrangement of plates.

Fossils at the base of the Cambrian are tiny. Some are teeth while others are fragments of a chain-mail type armour which is often spiny. Some of these chain-mail or cataphract animals, such as halkierids (2), are occasionally found whole. Slightly later skeletons tended to be more integrated, often with only one or two pieces, probably because they were better able to withstand predators equipped with tearing teeth. The evolution of predators may be one of the reasons for the development of hard parts. Changes in ocean chemistry close to the Precambrian–Cambrian boundary may also have facilitated the change, making the compounds from which skeletons are constructed, such as phosphates and calcium carbonate, more readily available.

The best records of Cambrian life are rare sites of exceptional fossil preservation such as the Burgess Shale, Canada (p.7), or the geologically older Chenjiang site in China. Initially, few species of animal existed, but through the Cambrian there was a rapid radiation of organisms, filling the many niches available on the ocean floor and in the water above. As this ecospace began to fill, more active competition developed between species. In comparison with the Precambrian period, the pace of change speeded up, with rapid rates of evolution and extinction. By the end of the Cambrian this recognisably modern state of affairs had developed, although the animals and plants inhabiting the ocean were very different from those of today.

Cambrian rocks in Britain are mainly confined to Wales, northern Scotland and small outcrops of rock in the Midlands. The most memorable Cambrian fossil is *Paradoxides*, an enormous trilobite up to 70 centimetres in length (3). Trilobites and other arthropods dominated the Cambrian faunas of Britain and the USA (1) while in warmer areas enormous reefs were built by primitive relatives of sponges known as archaeocyathids. Brachiopods, filter-feeding animals with two shells, snails and diverse groups of worms are also common from Cambrian rocks in Britain.

3 *Paradoxides davidis*, an enormous blind trilobite from Wales. This specimen is 45 cm long.

Lower Palaeozoic

Over geological time, we can trace the emergence and decline of fossil species and of the large and diverse ecosystems which they constructed. Three major faunas have dominated the seas through the last 550 million years (the Phanerozoic). The first of these was the Cambrian fauna which radiated so spectacularly when hard parts first evolved. The succeeding fauna dominated the Palaeozoic, suffering gradual extinction of its species and ending in the mass extinction event at the end of the Permian (p.36). This fauna was dominated by brachiopods, corals, cephalopods, and graptolites and was characterised by relatively simple food webs. The last of the three great evolutionary faunas arose after the Permian extinction event and dominates

the seas today. It is characterised by gastropods and bivalves, along with mammals, bony fishes, reptiles and echinoids (p.34).

Each of these faunas developed from stocks which were present in the earliest Cambrian. The earlier successful species radiated quickly, but also rapidly became extinct. Subsequent faunas arose and radiated later but were successful for much longer. It could be that rates of evolution were faster earlier in the evolution of metazoans because genetic instructions were simpler and easier to alter. Later organisms have had much less scope for radical changes in shape or body plan. Alternatively, the ever-increasing complexity of ecosystems may have made major innovations less and less likely as time has gone on.

Some of the first work on Lower Palaeozoic rocks was done in Britain. The outcrop of sediments of this age is extensive and the fossils are often beautifully preserved. A tradition of excellence in this field extends back over 150 years, to Sir Roderick Impey Murchison, who pioneered work on the Silurian system.

The Silurian is the third geological period of the Palaeozoic, and it is extremely well

2 *Amplexograptus maxwelli*, an Ordovician graptolite in an exceptional state of preservation, 3 mm long.

represented in the British Isles. Wales, southern Scotland and the mountains of the southern Lake District are made up of huge volumes of Silurian rock. It was a

Scotland

Iapetus Ocean

England & Wales

1 A map of Silurian Britain. The white patches indicate the extent of shallow-water reefs.

3 The Wenlock Limestone, a Silurian reef deposit from the Welsh borders, full of shells and coral debris.

period, 443–417 million years ago, when Britain was almost entirely covered by the sea, a time very different from the present. Scotland and England were separated from each other by the Iapetus ocean (p.13). Deeper water in northern England graded into shallower conditions and eventually to a patchy shoreline of islands across a line from the present Severn to the Humber (1). England was also at a very low latitude, effectively straddling the equator; thus its waters were teeming with life, warmed by the sun and fed with abundant nutrients from volcanic land areas to the north and south.

In the deeper water, life was dominated by graptolites (2). These are colonies of

5 A Silurian gastropod from the Wenlock limestone, *Horiostoma discors*.

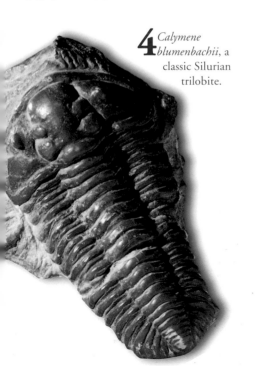

4 *Calymene blumenbachii*, a classic Silurian trilobite.

simple animals which together built skeletons of stunning regularity and complexity. Many different shapes of graptolite floated in the Silurian plankton, along with straight nautiloids, relatives of living *Nautilus*, and actively swimming trilobites. The best places to see these deep water deposits today are in mid-Wales, the Howgill Fells and the Southern Uplands of Scotland. At Dobs' Lin in Scotland a stream section exposes shales with abundant graptolites. The same sequence can be seen at Spengill in the Lake District and in the Rheidol Gorge of central Wales.

In shallower seas reefs flourished (3). These were mainly built up by calcareous algae, sponges and simple corals of the tabulate

and rugose groups. Around the reefs crawled dozens of species of trilobite (4) and gastropods (5), while crinoid and bryozoan thickets grew thickly along the reef margins and brachiopods nestled in crevices and clusters. The largest predators were eurypterids, sea scorpions up to two metres in length (6). These reef faunas were preserved in a belt which runs today from Gloucestershire up to Dudley, near Birmingham. The reef is named after Wenlock Edge in Shropshire, a long scarp which dominates the landscape of the Welsh Borders and is formed from the resistant limestone standing proud of the soft muds on either side.

6 *Eurypteris*, a sea scorpion from the Silurian of Scotland. This specimen is about 15 cm long.

Life onto land

Life evolved in the oceans, but we are most conscious of its diversity on land. The fossil record shows how life made the transition from one medium to another and conquered the terrestrial realm. New evidence shows that the transition began soon after the evolution of life. Precambrian soils 2000 million years old show traces of biological activity, a distinctive chemical signature left by photosynthesising bacteria, which demonstrates that the land has been occupied for much longer than was previously thought (1). The first multicellular organisms to invade the land were also photosynthesisers — simple plants. By the end of the Ordovician (443 million years ago) these plants had started to make the transition from freshwater to life on land. They probably began by colonising ephemeral ponds and wetlands. Gradually, more sophisticated adaptations allowed them to move further from standing water. The main obstacles to life on land involve desiccation, reproduction and support. The most successful group of modern plants have evolved woody tissue for support along with transport systems for moving water and nutrients, a protective coating broken by pores *(stomata)* for gas transfer, and reproductive spores which can survive desiccation. These are *vascular* plants. Mosses and liverworts (known together as *bryophytes*) have used an alternative strategy for land living which has inhibited their spread across dry ground.

Spores, which may belong to vascular plants or to bryophytes, are known from the Ordovician; the oldest fossils of vascular plants themselves are Silurian in age (425 million years old) and are known from many parts of the world, including Wales. The earliest vascular plant is called *Cooksonia* (2). It grew to about ten centimetres in height and had a simple branching shape with no leaves or roots. It lived only on low lying, wet, flood plains, but from these small beginnings diverse plants evolved quickly. By Devonian times (417 million years ago) vascular plants had become much more diverse, helping to produce soils and covering large areas of the land surface. As the Devonian progressed, plants became much more complicated, with leaves, roots and large size all developing. The first forests were home to a wide variety of insects, spiders and mites. The leaf litter was almost certainly burrowed by worms and provided a refuge for snails.

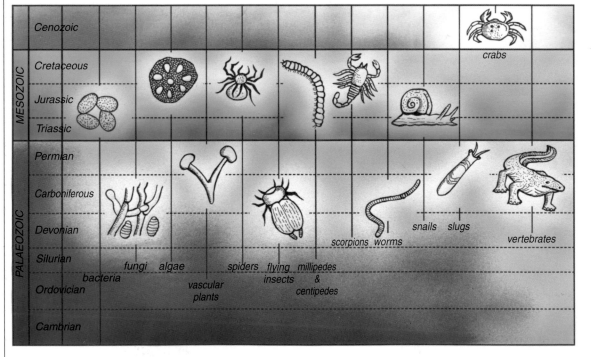

MESOZOIC	Cenozoic								crabs	
	Cretaceous									
	Jurassic									
	Triassic									
PALAEOZOIC	Permian									
	Carboniferous									
	Devonian									
	Silurian									
	Ordovician									
	Cambrian									

bacteria fungi algae vascular plants spiders flying insects millipedes & centipedes scorpions worms snails slugs vertebrates

1 The timing of colonisation of the land.

2 *Cooksonia*, the best known of the early vascular plants, which colonised the land in the Silurian.

Fungus had adapted to terrestrial life and played an important role in plant decay.

Vertebrates had also made the transition to life on land. In the Silurian, lungfish could probably drag themselves from the water to escape predators or to feed. The Devonian rock record yields the first reasonably complete and identifiable amphibians.

Large animals suffer many of the same problems of land living as do plants. They must undertake their own support, and elevate themselves off the ground in order to move around. They must also find a means of reproducing without releasing sperm and eggs directly into water. All of the early land vertebrates needed to return to water in order to reproduce. The fins of bony fish developed gradually into the limbs of early amphibians, with the necessary supports for the body being provided by pelvic and pectoral girdles. Interestingly, these early limbs ended in seven or eight toes rather than five.

The adaptation which most helped in the move onto land was probably the development of the *amniotic egg*. This protective capsule contains the fertilized egg and its food supply and can be laid on land. Reptiles with this critical terrestrial innovation appeared in the Carboniferous (354 million years ago), and the oldest specimen identified to date was found in 1991 in East Kirkton in Scotland (5).

By the Carboniferous many types of vascular plants formed tropical forests across the world. In these forests lived predatory reptiles and amphibians, flying and crawling insects (3, 4) along with millipedes longer and larger than dachsunds. The leaf litter was home to a variety of detritus feeders and scavengers, from fungi and worms to snails and larvae. The land was fully colonised, from soil layer to treetop canopy, and traces of these organisms are found across Britain within the coal-bearing strata in which they were buried.

4 *Hibbertopterus scouleri*, the largest scorpion in the world, from the Carboniferous of Scotland, 30 cm from claw to sting.

3 An extinct predatory spider, *Eophrynus*, from the Carboniferous, 4 cm long.

5 *Westlothiana lizziae*, probably a reptile and perhaps the first animal to lay eggs on land.

Plants and insects

Plants and insects have a history of interdependence which extends far back into the past. As time has gone on, the evolution of one group has stimulated evolution in the other so that they have become inextricably linked by a wide range of complicated adaptive strategies. This type of paired evolution in unrelated groups is of great interest to palaeontologists.

Structures which resemble animal burrows are found with the first Ordovician (450 million years ago) plant spores and suggest that plants and animals invaded the land at about the same time. A remarkable soil *lagerstätte* from the

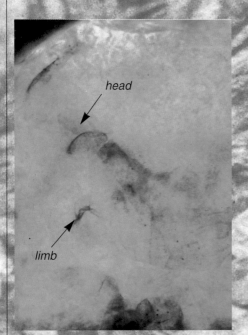

1 A primitive mite from the Devonian Rhynie Chert.

head

limb

2 Insect grazers have damaged these Cenozoic leaves, leaving bite marks on the margins.

Devonian (408 my) rocks of Rhynie in Northern Scotland provides a glimpse of this early plant community and the animals which fed on it (1).

The Rhynie rocks are a fossilised peat bog. This peat community thrived close to a volcanic hot spring which bled dissolved quartz into the ground water and caused the system to be petrified with every detail in place. The resulting fossils allow us to get an early picture of the interaction between plants and their predators. The plants of Rhynie are of a type which carried spores in chambers known as *sporangia*, prior to airborne dispersal. Within the petrified *sporangia* are tiny mites which were killed in the process of feeding on the spores. Slightly larger spiders and members of a group known as trigonotarbids are found preying on the mites. The mites themselves were somewhat protected whilst inside the sporangia. The Rhynie plants had spines on their stems, which may have acted to deter most mites from crawling up to the sporangia. However, they might also have helped the plant to conserve water, or served another, as yet unknown, function.

In Carboniferous (350 my) forests, plant spores were spread by feeding insects as they wandered through the trees. Insects achieved flight, the first animal group to do so, and the giant dragonflies of the Carboniferous forests probably preyed on the smaller winged insects of the tree canopy. Jurassic (200 my) plants of the *benititales* group developed strategies for attracting insects and beetles using smell or colour. The beetles, flies and wasps of the Mesozoic quickly responded to this new, edible, 'packaging'.

The most important phase in the relationship between plant and animal groups began in the Cretaceous (120 my) with the appearance of flowering plants or angiosperms. The seeds of angiosperms are protected in an ovary and fertilization occurs on the plant, when pollen is introduced to the protected egg. Flowers are the part of an angiosperm which hold the egg bearing ovule, and on which pollen must be seeded in order to produce fertilization. The first angiosperms are of early Cretaceous age and pollen of this period is found in the Weald area of England. Flowers similar to modern *Magnolia* are found from this time period in Russia and North America. The Weald Clay also contains pollinating beetles preserved with their colouration intact, as well as a range of other fossil insects.

The rise of flies and wasps, with mouthparts adapted to feed from these flowers, occurred soon after the evolution of the flowers themselves. Since that time, the progressive specialization of some flowers and the feeding apparatus of their pollinators suggests that coevolution may be at

work, although it is an impossible concept to prove beyond all doubt.

Overall, the level of plant-insect interaction has increased many fold since

4 A beautifully preserved Cretaceous dragonfly *Valdaeshna surreyensis* from southern England.

the evolution of angiosperms. Feeding on all parts of the plants (2, 3), and the use of plants for protection or shelter became common in the Cretaceous, although known from much older forests. Angiosperms, with their broad leaves, may make insect damage easier to see in fossils, but it also seems that they have been part of an ongoing development in the relationship between the plant and animal kingdoms.

3 Boring and burrowing has left large holes in this Cenozoic leaf.

Vertebrates

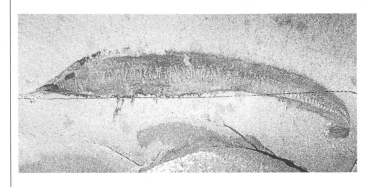

1 *Pikaia*, probably a swimming predator, is an ancestor of vertebrates, from the Cambrian Burgess Shale of Canada.

Vertebrates are an ancient group of animals with an enormously flexible body plan. With a head, bilateral symmetry, and a dorsal nerve chord, they have developed into the most influential group of animals on the planet. They have colonised the sea and freshwater as well as land and the air. They are a group which includes fishes and amphibians, reptiles, birds and mammals. The history of their evolution is our own story.

Vertebrates evolved in the Precambrian, and their oldest preserved remains are Cambrian (550 my) in age. The Burgess Shale (p.24) of Canada contains an ancestral vertebrate called *Pikaia* (1), with many of the features of the living group. The earliest fish are also Cambrian in age, but are found in fragments because only external bony plates are preserved as fossils: their skeletons must have been made from cartilage rather than bone. These early fish lacked jaws, which are first seen in fossils from the Silurian period (438 my). Jaws evolved at the same time in several evolutionary lines, including those leading to bony fish (2), like herring, and the cartilaginous sharks.

It may have been a bony fish, like the 'living fossil' *Coelocanth*, which first made the transition to life on land in the Devonian period. The oldest amphibians are found in Greenland and date from uppermost Devonian time. Although they are so old, *Ichthyostega* and *Acanthostega* have many advanced characteristics and are not the ancestors of the rest of the later vertebrates. They were probably water dwellers and some features of their skulls suggest that they breathed with gills. Their strong limbs were used for swimming but were pre-adapted for moving around on the land. Land-dwelling amphibians became abundant by the Carboniferous, as they occupied a range of terrestrial niches (3). An exceptional find from Scotland, and another from Nova Scotia, preserve a range of animals including agile insectivores, large predators and limbless, snake-like forms. The Scottish find also contains the oldest reptile, *Westlothiana lizzae* (p.29)

The evolutionary step between amphibians and reptiles is vital to the later evolution of the vertebrates. Reptiles lay eggs which are surrounded by a waterproof membrane and can be left to develop on dry land. This amniotic egg allowed reptiles to colonise many drier and higher habitats, away from standing water. Two major types of amniotic egg-bearing reptile arose very early in their evolutionary history. One of these lines gave rise to mammals, the other to dinosaurs and birds. The early mammal-like reptiles evolved in the Permian and thrived in the Triassic, when advanced predators, such as *Thrinaxodon*, roamed across southern

2 This Jurassic fossil, *Pholidophorus bechei*, is a beautiful example of a bony fish.

3 *Balanerpeton*, a terrestrial amphibian from the Carboniferous of Scotland.

Africa and the other southern landmasses. However, following extinctions towards the end of the Triassic, the proto-mammals were eclipsed by a group of reptiles from the other major adaptive line — the dinosaurs.

Dinosaurs were diverse and widespread, dominating the land masses of the Mesozoic world. They evolved into complicated ecosystems with grazers and predators. Some developed social behaviour such as herding and returned each year to preferred nesting sites. They grew to be the largest land animals the world has seen, and the most fearsome predators. As children, our imagination is fuelled by visions of lumbering herds of *Apatosaurus*, the giant killer *Tyrannosaurus* and the rhino-like *Triceratops* (4). Similarly haunting is their fate — a gradual decline through the Cretaceous, terminating in extinction, probably after a giant meteorite impacted into the Yucatan area of Mexico (p.37).

Some people have suggested that dinosaurs were warm blooded and this must be a likely possibility,

4 *Triceratops*, one of the best known of the dinosaurs.

considering the fact that they gave rise to warm blooded descendents — the birds. The oldest bird, *Archaeopteryx*, comes from the Solnhofen Limestone in Germany (p.6–7). But for its possession of feathers, it is identical to a small dinosaur called *Compsognathus*. Although dinosaurs had developed the ability to fly, it is the birds that have truly colonised the air. The early birds were unaffected by the end-Cretaceous extinction and radiated throughout the Cretaceous and Cenozoic.

After the demise of the last dinosaurs, the mammals began to evolve with astonishing speed. From a small, omnivorous ancestor, a myriad of different mammal lineages developed. Ten million years after the last dinosaur, the world had been recolonised with mammals — predators, grazers (5), water dwellers and bats. The earliest horses roamed the new, arid plains of Africa, and in the trees were the earliest primates, an evolutionary lineage leading to man.

5 *Arsinoitherium*, a 35 million year old rhinoceras-like mammal from Egypt.

Mesozoic

A dinosaur discovered in southern England or a marine reptile from a Cotswold quarry become news items to fire the imagination. They take us back in time to the Mesozoic, when Britain was part of a tropical paradise crawling with new and dangerous forms of life.

The Mesozoic spans the period of time between the great extinctions at the end of the Permian and Cretaceous, from 248 to 65 million years ago. It is divided into three periods, Triassic, Jurassic and Cretaceous. On land, these periods witnessed the rise and ultimate demise of dinosaurs, along with the evolution of birds, mammals and flowering plants (page 30–31). In the sea, the great

2 A Jurassic belemnite preserved with the guard and the phragmocone intact.

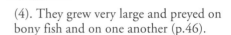

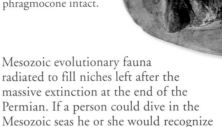

Mesozoic evolutionary fauna radiated to fill niches left after the massive extinction at the end of the Permian. If a person could dive in the Mesozoic seas he or she would recognize many modern forms of life, and see others which are absent today.

3 *Pentacrinus*, in a mass of crinoid heads and stems from the Jurassic of Lyme Regis.

Shallow sea beds around Britain were covered by crinoid thickets (3) and reefs while muddy areas were dominated by gastropods and bivalves. Belemnites (2) and ammonites (1) are the commonest fossils found from deeper, offshore deposits. Marine reptiles were common in the seas and in lakes

(4). They grew very large and preyed on bony fish and on one another (p.46).

Most rocks which are exposed in England across the Cotswolds, Chilterns, Wolds, up to North Yorkshire and into the Home Counties, are of Mesozoic age. There are also many more scattered outcrops in Northern Ireland and in the Western Isles of Scotland. Most of these rocks are sediments — sandstones, shales and limestones, which were laid down in a shallow shelf sea. At times, Britain was a landmass, but in general the Mesozoic was a time of high sea levels, when the continental shelves were much wider than they are now (6).

The archetypal locality for British Jurassic fossils is Lyme Regis in Dorset. Mary Anning collected there in the 19th

4 A Lyme Regis ichthyosaur, a small marine predatory reptile.

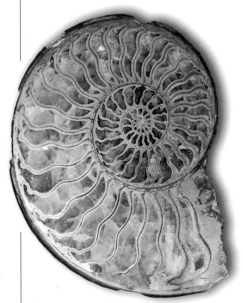

1 *Oxynoticeras lymense*, a characteristic ammonite from Lyme Regis.

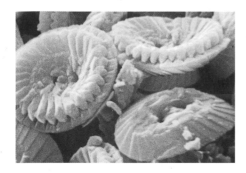

5 Coccoliths, the remains of planktic plants which make up the Chalk.

century, and every cliff fall reveals a trove of fresh and beautifully preserved fossils. The rocks in this area were laid down in quiet, deep waters during the early Jurassic. Deposition was slow, and clays, lime muds and silts settled on the bottom under calm conditions to form banded mudstones. Very little oxygen was present

at or below the sea bed, so organisms decayed very slowly, assisting their preservation as fossils.

The white cliffs of Dover are another familiar symbol of Mesozoic Britain. They are made of chalk and were deposited during the later part of the Cretaceous period. Chalk is a rock made entirely from fossils; the microscopic skeletons of planktic plants called coccolithophorids (5) make up the lime mud of the chalk. Flints, scattered thickly within certain layers, are made from silica which originally belonged to sponges and to microscopic plankton. The Chalk Sea would have had a muddy floor: it might have been possible to sink through thick mud for tens of metres before coming to rest on anything solid. Animals could only thrive if they had a burrowing lifestyle or if they had 'snowshoe' adaptations to keep them afloat on the soft mud. Burrowing echinoids (7) and free-swimming ammonites are the most common large fossils in the chalk, along with flattened or spiny bivalves (8). Unfortunately, the seas withdrew from Britain before the end of the Cretaceous, so that evidence of the end of dinosaurs and ammonites is missing from the British rock record.

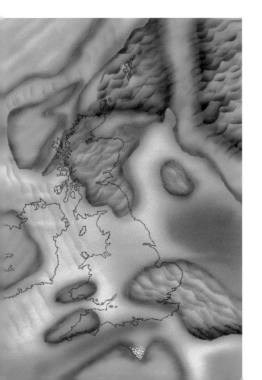

6 The Jurassic geography of Britain.

7 *Micraster*, a burrowing Cretaceous sea urchin (echinoid).

8 *Spondylus spinosus*, a bivalve with spines to prevent it sinking into the chalk mud.

Mass extinctions

Many times in the geological past, the world's compliment of plants and of animals have been exposed to crises which have threatened their existence. Dinosaurs, ammonites and trilobites died out as a result of these mass extinctions.

A mass extinction is brought on by changes in the Earth's climate, which are too extreme for most organisms to survive, and too rapid to allow them time to adapt. The rocks record a dramatic decline in the number of species inhabiting a range of ecological niches. Land dwellers and ocean

1 The pattern of mass extinctions over the last 300 my. The two most catastrophic are at the end of the Permian and at the end of the Cretaceous.

2 *Calymene blumenbachii,* ▶ a trilobite curled in a defensive position.

plankton, plants and carnivores, are all affected at the same time.

Arguments rage about the possible causes of mass extinctions. The fossil record seems to show that extinctions occur regularly: they are not randomly distributed in geological time but occur roughly every 26 million years (1). If mass extinctions are regular, then perhaps an extraterrestrial cause is to blame. Alternatively, irregular terrestrial events may be responsible, such as volcanic eruptions or changes in sea level. A third

3 *Eurypterus* ▲ *nanus.* All sea scorpions became extinct at the end of the Permian.

possible cause is biological. The present is undoubtedly a time of mass extinction, mediated by man's effect on the planet. Other innovations of life through time, from the introduction of oxygen into the atmosphere to the appearance of grass, could have produced similar results.

The two most dramatic catastrophes in the history of life were the extinctions at the end of the Permian and at the end of the Cretaceous. The end Permian extinction was the biggest crisis experienced by multicelled life; it is estimated that 96 % of marine invertebrate species became extinct at this time. The Palaeozoic fauna (p. 26) was devastated, with the demise of trilobites (2), eurypterids (3), and tabulate and

Graph: Families extinct (%) vs Millions of years before present. Labels: "End-Permian event", "End-Cretaceous event".

rugose corals. Simultaneously, on land, animals and plants suffered a major series of extinctions.

The causes of this extinction were almost certainly terrestrial in origin. The end of the Permian was a time when all of the continents were assembled into a single supercontinent, we call *Pangaea*, which straddled the equator. As a result, the climate became much more extreme, sea levels fell and the amount of shallow seafloor declined drastically. Extinction in most groups took several million years, and is recorded in the relatively gradual decline in diversity towards the end of the period.

This compares dramatically with the extinction at the end of the Cretaceous. This is the best known of all mass

4 *Androgynoceras artigyrus.* Ammonites became extinct at the end of the Cretaceous.

extinctions because it saw the end of both ammonites (4) and dinosaurs (5). The effects of this event were recorded best by microfossils, which show what happened to ecosystems across the globe at this time. The best preserved section across the end-Cretaceous bondary is at El Kef in Tunisia, but the pattern seen there is repeated in rocks preserved beneath the world's oceans. In all cases the extinction horizon in the rocks comes as an abrupt event terminating a prolonged period of decline.

The probable cause of extinction at the end of the Cretaceous is the impact of comets or asteroids. The boundary is marked by a many-fold increase in the quantity of iridium in clays, an element rare on the earth's surface but more

5 *Gasosaurus.* A dinosaur skeleton.

common in meteorites. Quartz grains which have been shocked by massive pressures are found at this horizon as are tektites, molten spheres of rock and mineral typical of impact events and nuclear tests. The greatest concentration of shocked quartz is in North America, and the most likely candidate for an impact site is the huge meteor crater of Chicxulub hidden under the forests of Yucatan in Central America. Although the exact sequence of events following a large impact is unknown, it is clear that dust and gases released into the atmosphere would have had a devastating effect on planetary climate for several thousands of years.

Cenozoic

The last 65 million years have seen the evolution and radiation of modern life-forms, from elephants to mussels, wheat to whales. These forms evolved from the survivors of the mass extinction at the end of the Cretaceous period (p. 36–37) and have become the complicated ecosystems of the present world.

These survivors faced two major challenges as they began to explore the empty ecospace of the land and oceans. Firstly, climatic changes were beginning to occur, which have culminated in our present Ice Age. Secondly, enormous earth movements built mountains, dried seas and moved continents, alternately separating and uniting areas with profoundly different ecosystems. As a result of these geological forces, the history of life in the Cenozoic has recorded a series of extinctions and minor crises, with the dominant organisms in one area migrating or dying as conditions changed.

The major radiations of life in the Cenozoic occurred within this context of

cooling and upheaval. On land the most important groups to radiate were mammals and large, flightless birds. In the seas, molluscs came to dominate the sea floor, and bony fish the waters above.

The beginning of the Cenozoic was a warm time, with widespread and regular rainfall. Few areas had marked seasons, and semi-tropical vegetation extended to the poles. The early mammals were adapted to this dense woodland cover, and were mainly small and omnivorous.

With continents on the move, different parts of the world experienced different evolutionary pathways, such that marsupials developed in the isolated southern continents. As the climate began to

1 The head of a rare, toothed bird, *Odontopteryx toliapicus*, from the London Clay.

cool, weather patterns became more seasonal. This had the effect of reducing the intensity of forest vegetation, allowing more niches, at different heights above ground, to be exploited. The diversity of niches occupied by mammals expanded, with the evolution of specialized grazers, carnivores, sea dwellers and flyers.

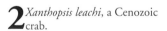

2 *Xanthopsis leachi*, a Cenozoic crab.

The temperature peak for the Cenozoic came about 38 million years ago. Then temperatures began to fall rapidly. By the end of the Eocene (34 million years ago) frost began to affect high latitudes. All over the world climates became drier and more seasonal. Forests died back and many mammals became extinct as their food supply waned. As Asia and Europe became linked by land, a wave of extinctions followed the westward

3 A bony fish, *Scombrinus nuchalis*, from the rocks below London.

4 A generalized geography of late Cenozoic Britain.

migration of Asian mammals. During the Miocene, sea levels fell as water became trapped in the growing ice caps of Antarctica and Greenland. At the same time, the mountain ranges of western North America, the Andes and Himalayas began to rise very rapidly. This caused climatic cooling and drying, followed by another wave of extinction.

Around ten million years ago, a seminal evolutionary event occurred, which has changed the face of much of the world's land surface. Grasses evolved, ideally suited to seasonal and dry conditions. Their spread at the expense of forests radically altered temperate and semitropical ecosystems. The modern savannah grazers evolved at this time, along with large, swift carnivores well adapted to giving chase across the open countryside.

In Britain, most rocks of Cenozoic age are found in the south

east, and in the highlands and islands of Scotland. At the beginning of the Cenozoic, the sea covered the area south east of a line from the Chilterns to Dorset. The clay on which London is built contains a wealth of marine and terrestrial fossils (1, 2, 3), and shows that the land was tropical and forested, the sea warm and full of life. As time went on, the sea withdrew from most of the country (4), and the patches where deposition continued, such as the Suffolk coast, show a cooling climate and the extinction of many groups. However, as recently as three million years ago, coral colonies thrived in the North Sea (5, 6). They, along with so many other temperate and tropical species, were killed off by the onset of widespread glaciation about 1.8 million years ago.

5 *Flabellum woodi*, a colonial coral which lived in the North Sea about three million years ago.

6 *Cryptangis woodi*, a solitary coral from the Coralline Crag in Norfolk.

The evolution of man

Few topics introduce political and moral concerns into fossil studies as does the search for human origins. Yet it is also one of the most important fields of palaeontology. It is natural and vital for a curious species to investigate its own beginnings. This is no easy task. For most of our history, humans and their ancestors have been scarce animals. Living on land, and having skeletons which fell apart in decay, made them even more unlikely candidates for the fossil record. Human remains are thus uncommon and fragmentary so that arguments rage which are based on the features of a mere handful of incomplete bones.

Fossil primates are found in the rock record from about 55 million years ago. The hominoids, a group which includes the great apes (orangutans, chimpanzees and gorillas) as well as modern man, became recognizeable around 17 million years ago and the final split between the line leading to man and to the living apes occurred about five million years ago. This split occurred in Africa at a time of increasingly dry climate and global cooling, when tropical forests were succeeded by wooded grassland.

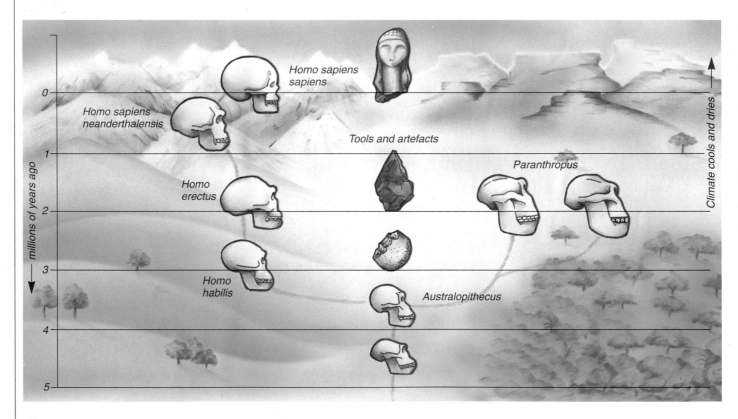

1 A simplified pattern of the evolution of hominids. Such interpretations change with every major new find.

2 Skulls of early and modern man in chronological order left to right: *Australopithecus*; *Homo habilis*; *Homo erectus*; two Neanderthal skulls *(Homo sapiens neanderthalensis)*; Modern man *(Homo sapiens sapiens)*.

These climatic changes may have sparked the rapid evolution of hominid stocks.

The fossil record of hominids is very sparse until about 3.5 million years ago (1). At this time we can recognise *Australopithecus afarensis* (2), an erect and relatively large-brained hominid, which gave rise to at least two lineages, the groups *Paranthropus* and *Homo* (1). By two million years ago two species of *Paranthropus* existed alongside the first species of the genus *Homo*, *Homo habilis*, which had a brain about 45% larger than its *Paranthropus* relatives. Some or all of these species were tool makers, but *Homo habilis* carried the process to a much more sophisticated level. These hominid species slowly began to spread out beyond Africa, and *Homo habilis* evolved into *Homo erectus* and eventually into *Homo sapiens* through small, gradual changes in shape. European remains of *Homo erectus* are

known from rare and widely scattered sites. Hominids faced a great climatic challenge in invading northern Europe as ice was advancing and retreating in great sweeps across much of Britain, Ireland, the Alps, Spain and Scandinavia. Sophisticated social cooperation and practical skills would have been necessary for survival. Populations of *H.erectus* were gradually replaced about 70 000 years ago by the migration of recognizably modern *Homo sapiens*. The earliest sub-species of *Homo sapiens* seen on this icy fringe of Northern Europe was *H.sapiens neanderthalensis*, or Neanderthal man. This group too was replaced, by modern man, around 30 000 years ago.

Human remains in Britain are patchy. A partial skull of *Homo*

erectus is known from Swanscombe in Kent, and a recent and important find of bones has been made at Boxgrove in Sussex. However, the tools which were made and used by fossil hominids are much more common than their bones, and yield much more information about the colonisation of Britain (3).

3 A leaf-like knife from Cambridgeshire.

Ice ages

For two and a half million years, the Northern hemisphere has been intermittently buried under enormous ice sheets. The process has not stopped, but at present we are in an interglacial period when the ice sheets are in decline. The animals and plants of the ice age world adapted well to the cold and record the sequence of ice advances and retreats; but many could not survive the impact of hunting and their fossil record shows the first mass extinction caused by man.

Ice has been accumulating in Antarctica for at least 38 million years, but for reasons we do not completely understand, ice suddenly swept south across the northern hemisphere two million years ago. Ice sheets, kilometres thick, built up over a period of perhaps 10 000 years, covering most of North America, Europe, the Middle East, and northern Asia (2). The ocean was drained of the water locked into the ice and sea levels fell by about 120 metres.

1 The tooth of a warm climate elephant (*Anancus arvernensis*) preserved from an interglacial period in Britain during which temperatures were higher than at present.

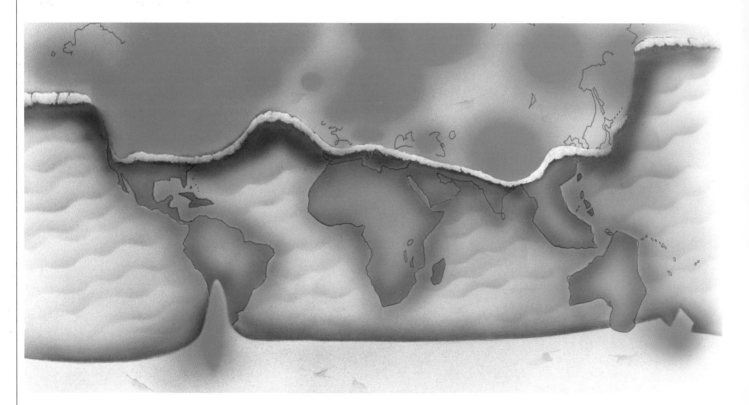

2 The world under ice. Falls in sea level during glacial advances made land bridges, such as those between the islands of Indonesia.

3 An Irish Elk.

front of an invading ice sheet was cut off. Many warm water molluscs became trapped in a cooling North Sea and died out. The Irish elk (3), a deer with antlers three metres across, became trapped in Ireland during the last advance around 11 000 years ago and died there, unable to migrate further south because of the flooding of land routes to Britain. Man reached Ireland about 8000 years ago.

In many areas, but especially in the New World, many large herbivores became extinct over a short time period about 11 000 years ago. In North America, over 50 species of mammal, including sabre tooth tigers, camels, mammoths and giant ground sloths, were all lost. Although the timing of their demise coincides with a period of rapid climatic change, such changes had been experienced before,

without a significant loss of faunas. What other factor could have caused this? Just over 11 000 years ago, the Bering land bridge joined up to an ice free corridor along the western seaboard of America, admitting man into the New World from Asia for the first time. Experienced in hunting, he found a rich wildlife unused to man and slaughtered it. The large mammals like mammoths, which bred slowly, had no chance of escaping, or recovering from, this predation. Overkill of these animals would have changed the open nature of the grasslands, making the grass tougher and thicker and excluding smaller grazers. Large predators would have suffered as their natural prey disappeared.

In the Old World, large mammals survived predation for much longer, but during the last glacial retreat they gradually became confined to a few refuges and were then hunted out of those into extinction. In Britain, cave deposits preserve abundant remains of hyenas (4), mammoths and woolly rhinos, which were over-hunted as the last ice retreated.

Once ice has formed, its advances and retreats are controlled by small variations in the Earth's orbit, known as *Milankovitch cycles*, which cause tiny changes in the amount of incoming heat from the sun. As the ice has advanced and retreated, animals and plants have been driven before it.

Animals followed the migration of their food, and the glacial world was dominated by large mammals like mammoths and woolly rhinos. Enormous flightless birds thrived on the island continents of Australasia and South America. Extinctions seem to have occurred when the line of retreat from the

4 Lower jaw of a cave hyena, *Crocuta crocuta*, from Derbyshire.

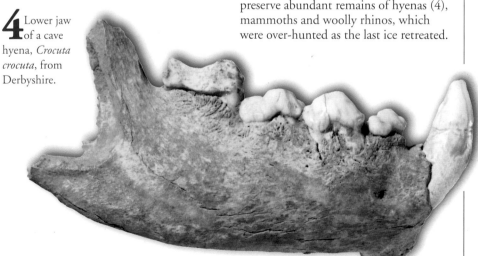

Case studies

Six case studies show how fossils are being studied at the cutting edge of science. They give a flavour of the variety of techniques which can be used, and the spectacular results which can be achieved by modern palaeontology.

1 The fate of a Jurassic forest

Along the Dorset coast are outcrops of a late Jurassic fossil forest. For many years it posed a conundrum for palaeontologists because the trees are found amongst rocks which must have formed in salty lagoons, where modern trees would die. The botanical investigation of these trees was undertaken by Dr Jane Francis at the University of Leeds.

The Purbeck fossil forests at Lulworth Cove and on the Isle of Portland were made up of large trees. The stumps which have been preserved reach almost two metres in diameter (1) and are spaced 3–5 metres apart. This indicates a deeply forested region, with a full tree canopy. Most of the trees were of one type, a shallow rooting conifer belonging to an extinct family. Their leaves had thick cuticles which would have helped conserve water in a dry environment.

The soil in which the fossil forest grew was well drained and lay close to a marine lagoon. Evaporation caused a layer in the soil to become hardened like natural cement and this probably trapped freshwater near the surface within reach of the shallow roots. The fossil conifer

1 A tree stump from the Purbeck fossil forest, Dorset.

trunks have growth rings, showing that they grew seasonally and were dormant for part of each year. In dry areas today, the season of growth is when rain is most frequent. The tree rings are of uneven width and sometimes show a cessation of growth in mid season; the trees were

sensitive to changes in their environment, often experiencing restricted growth as a result of unexpected water shortage.

The fossil forest died when sea levels rose, flooding their roots with saline water. Marine algae grew around their decaying trunks and preserved them as fossils. Seasonal changes in the salinity of the lagoon allowed chert to replace some of the wood, petrifying it in exquisite detail. By comparing these well-preserved remains with modern plants and modern environments, this work demonstrates that the climate in the south of England during the late Jurassic was dry, hot and highly seasonal, with extreme variations in rainfall between seasons and unpredictible droughts occurring every few years.

2 How early man killed his prey

The butchered bones of large mammals from the campsites of early man show the ways in which these animals were captured and killed. The method of study involves entire populations, rather than information from only one individual.

The method for assessing the cause of death of butchered animals originates in the study of populations of animals suffering different causes of mortality in natural settings. At Langebaanweg in South Africa, large mammals are well preserved in the sediments of an early Pliocene river. Four species are present, giraffe, rhino, cow and long-necked antelope. The bones of each species show an individual's age at death, and the

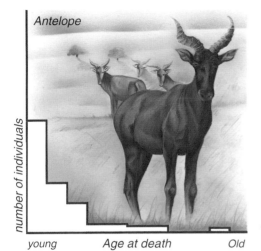

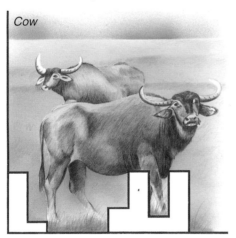

2 The age distribution of dead individuals for four species of grassland grazer.

reconstruction of patterns of mortality shows how the animal groups died (2).

The giraffe and the long-necked antelope show an age distribution with all members of the population represented. Young ones are most abundant, but mature adults and old individuals are also present. This is the same distribution as would be seen in a census of a modern population. Thus the fossilised remains represent a snapshot of the living population—all of the individuals were killed at the same time by a sudden catastrophe. In this case a flash flood in the river is the most likely cause of death. By contrast, the rhinocerous and the cow remains have a very different pattern. Young and old individuals are well represented, but mature adults are rare or absent. This is similar to the age distribution of bodies in a graveyard, where the population is built up over time by the 'natural' deaths of the unfit or unwell. For the river bed bones, the distribution pattern suggests a gradual build-up of dead animals carried by the river waters and left on sand bars, rather than the sudden death of a herd.

The Langebaanweg bones show two patterns of mortality which are also found in the bones recovered from hominid sites across the world. Where a mass mortality is recorded, similar to the distribution pattern for giraffes and antelopes, then it can be inferred that early man was able to kill an entire herd of animals at one go. Herds were driven over cliffs or into ravines for slaughter. Where an attritional mortality profile is seen, as for the South African rhinos and cows, it can be inferred that the animals were hunted individually, with the old and the very young most likely to be caught by hunters. By comparing natural and butchered populations, this study provides a tool for interpreting the hunting patterns of our distant ancestors before the onset of domestication about 12 000 years ago.

Case studies

3 Food chains in the Jurassic seas

The Oxford Clay is a marine deposit of Middle Jurassic age which crops out in a diagonal line across England running from Weymouth north-east to Scarborough. It is extensively quarried for brickmaking, so that there are large and frequently renewed exposures along the length of the outcrop. Fish, ammonites and shells of all types are common fossils. Dr Dave Martill and colleagues have studied the fossils of the Oxford Clay to determine the food chains in this ancient sea.

Ecology is difficult to investigate in fossils, because it constitutes a description of the interaction between living organisms. To study fossils in this way means using data from several sources: looking at the functional adaptations of fossils, comparing fossils with similar modern organisms, studying the way in which they are

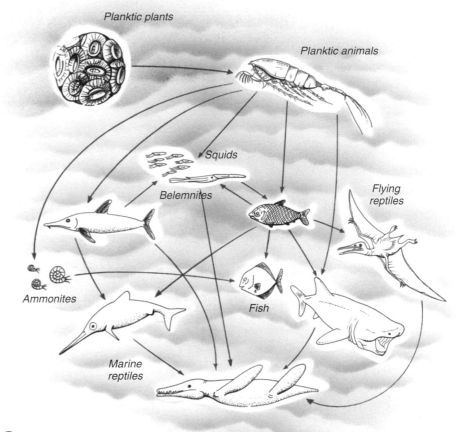

2 The web of interactions between swimming and floating organisms in the Jurassic seas.

1 Bite marks on this plesiosaur leg bone indicate that it was preyed on as well as being a predator itself.

preserved, and examining the frequency with which sets of fossils co-occur. By using all of these techniques, Martill and his colleagues have revealed a complicated ecology with highly specialised interactions between organisms (2).

The water from which the Oxford Clay was deposited was warm, at about 21° C, and about 80 metres deep. The seabed was muddy and most bottom dwellers rested gingerly on its sloppy

surface. Bivalves of all types were common on the sea bed, mostly feeding from the nutrients in the clay. Small brittle stars nestled in the shell thickets and scavenged scraps of food.

In the upper layers of the water large marine reptiles cruised for prey, including the 10 metres long pliosaur *Liopleurodon ferox* (1). Crocodiles, too, were common in the surface waters, and fed on the abundant scaly fish and on ammonites.

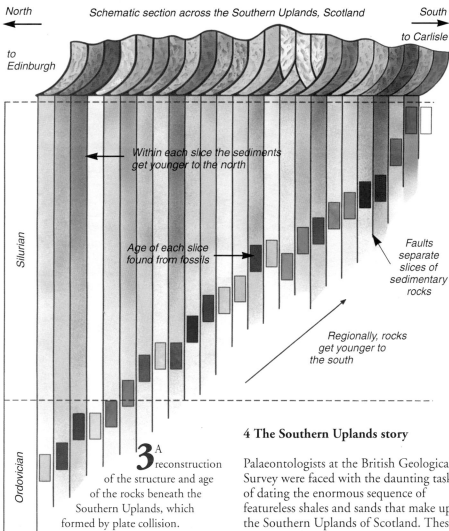

North ← Schematic section across the Southern Uplands, Scotland   **South** →

to Edinburgh

to Carlisle

Within each slice the sediments get younger to the north

Age of each slice found from fossils →

Silurian

Ordovician

Faults separate slices of sedimentary rocks

Regionally, rocks get younger to the south

3 A reconstruction of the structure and age of the rocks beneath the Southern Uplands, which formed by plate collision.

Rarer, but more dramatic, was the enormous plankton-feeding fish, *Leedsichthys*, which may have reached 20 metres in length. All of these feeders were ultimately sustained by the billions of tiny planktic plants which bloomed in the warm surface waters, fixing energy direct from the sun.

4 The Southern Uplands story

Palaeontologists at the British Geological Survey were faced with the daunting task of dating the enormous sequence of featureless shales and sands that make up the Southern Uplands of Scotland. These rocks are of Ordovician and Silurian age and were deposited in a marine environment. Graptolites are common in the shales, and are of great use in dating rocks of this age.

Detailed biostratigraphy of these Scottish rocks has thown new light on how they formed, and on the plate tectonic setting of this part of Scotland 450 million years ago.

Case studies

The rocks of the Southern Uplands are known to be divided by a series of south-west-trending faults. Fossils from these fault slices reveal an intriguing pattern in the rocks. In each fault slice the sequence begins with shales and ends with sands. Each slice shows rocks which get younger towards the north, but as a whole the set of faulted rocks gets younger to the south. This pattern can be determined because of the precise dating possible through graptolites (3).

How can the earth's movements produce a stack of rocks which form from north to south, but between faults has rocks which formed from south to north? The answer is to be found in modern settings like the Indonesian area of SE Asia. Deep below the sea floor of the Indian Ocean, a plate of oceanic crust is sinking towards the east below continental Indonesia. As it sinks, the sediments of the Bengal submarine plain are scraped off the top and added to the Indonesian continent in a stacked set of fault bounded slices. Each slice is stacked onto the continent on its edge, with the youngest top facing onshore. However, subsequent fault slices are stacked outboard of earlier ones, so, as a whole, the set of faulted rocks becomes younger towards the sea.

Four hundred and fifty million years ago, southern Scotland sat above the leading edge of a north-descending piece of oceanic crust, which separated England from Scotland (p.13). As this crust sank into the mantle, sediments were scraped off to form this *accretionary prism*, in exactly the same way as in Indonesia today.

Case studies

5 What are conodonts?

Tiny, tooth-like fossils, known as conodonts (1), are common in rocks of Cambrian to Triassic age. They have proved to be excellent in dating rocks, and they also change colour when heated, precisely recording their depth of burial inside the Earth. However, the nature of the animal from which conodonts came, even the function of the conodonts themselves, was unknown until 1982. Since then a revolution in our understanding of conodonts has put them in the forefront of research into the origins of vertebrates, the group to which we belong.

In the collections of the British Geological Survey in Edinburgh are fossils from the Carboniferous Granton Shrimp Bed. A researcher noticed conodonts on a slab of Shrimp Bed, still attached to the soft parts of a slender, eel-like animal. The conodonts were teeth, placed in the head of the animal just below two large eyes. Ten specimens have now been found, each about four centimetres in length. In 1994, Dr Dick Aldridge and colleagues at the University of Leicester also found a giant conodont animal, ten times as large, in Ordovician rocks from South Africa. The conodont animal has large eyes, a thin body with V-shaped muscles, an axial stiffening rod (effectively a primitive backbone) and tail fins. These features place it on the evolutionary line to vertebrates. The composition of the conodont teeth themselves make this relationship even closer. New techniques suggest that they are made of a combination of enamel, dentine and bone found only in vertebrates.

The importance of this discovery is enormous. The oldest conodonts are at least 30 million years older than any other vertebrate and the first to produce hard parts— teeth. Older views on the origin of hard parts predicted that they began as defensive, armoured plates protecting prey animals. However, it now looks as though hard parts originated for attack. The first vertebrates were active predators rather than prey. Luck, skill and detective work into the nature of conodonts has led to new evidence for the origin and early evolution of our vertebrate lineage.

6 The temperature of the sea

The calcite skeletons of fossils can be used to give a chemical insight into the conditions in which they lived. Planktic fossils record the temperature of the surface waters of the sea, while bottom dwelling organisms record temperatures on the sea bed. The vertical variation in sea temperature, and its overall temperature, can both be used as climatic indicators and can pick out those times in the past when ice was present and those times when it was absent.

The most useful organisms for a study such as this are foraminiferans (2), microscopic animals which build a chambered skeleton out of calcite (calcium carbonate, or $CaCO_3$). Today

1 Conodonts, the teeth of primitive vertebrates.

48

2 A microscopic foraminifera. These tiny animals live at all water depths and record sea temperatures in the composition of their skeletons.

they live in all of the world's oceans, and they were even more abundant in the past than they are now. They inhabit all levels of the water column from surface to sea bed, and their life position is recorded by a characteristic shell shape. It is not their shells, or even the calcite with which they are built, but the nature of the oxygen molecules in that calcite that gives an accurate record of temperature.

Oxygen occurs in two natural isotopes, ^{18}O and ^{16}O. Isotopes are atoms of a single element which can have a variable number of neutrons in its central core: ^{18}O has ten neutrons, ^{16}O has eight and so is slightly lighter. As water evaporates from the sea surface the lighter isotope

evaporates more rapidly than the heavier one. At times when the temperature is low and ice locks water onto land, the seas become depleted in ^{16}O and enriched in ^{18}O. This balance is redressed when ice melts. Foraminifera take oxygen from sea water and record the isotopic ratio of the time when they constructed their skeletons. This data can be retrieved by palaeontologists using a mass spectrometer, and the results plotted to show temperature changes through time.

Over the last 140 million years, the foraminifera of the north Pacific record

two things: an overall cooling in water temperature, and an increasing difference between the surface and bottom water temperatures. Over time the bottom waters have cooled more rapidly because they originate from the poles and flow towards the equator under the warmer surface waters. The increasing divergence reflects the gradient of surface temperature with increasing latitude, and shows the rapid cooling of the poles and slower cooling of the equatorial regions as the Earth entered the present Ice Age.

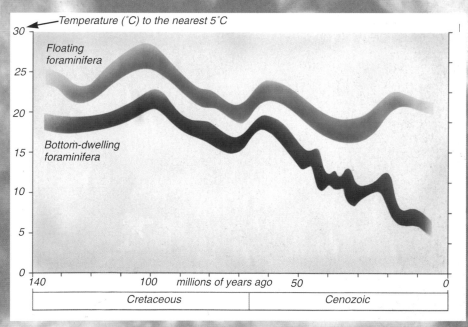

3 The temperature of surface and deep sea water over the last 140 million years, north Pacific.

The great collectors

Fossils have been collected since prehistoric times, but their significance, and their origin from living organisms, has only been understood in the last few centuries. The interpretations of fossils and their meaning has mirrored the larger development of thought and the changing view of the universe held by man.

During the Middle Ages, fossils were thought to originate within the Earth and to be evidence for the creative processes latent underground. Collections of fossils were made throughout this time, but they only survive as illustrations in books.

In parallel with the theory of spontaneous formation of fossils, and outlasting it, was the idea that fossils had been deposited in

their present positions by a universal deluge, perhaps by Noah's flood (1). This was assumed to have occurred in the recent past as a single catastrophic episode. The period of greatest acceptance for this idea in Britain was during the late 17th and early 18th centuries, and one of its strongest exponents was John Woodward (1665–1728). His intact collection of fossils and other natural objects is preserved in the Sedgwick Museum in Cambridge (background facing page).

As the Renaissance transformed thought, the true nature of fossils began to be understood, first on mainland Europe and subsequently in Britain. Leonardo da Vinci (1452–1519) recognised that fossils were the remains of organisms, and invoked the occurrence of shells on the sea shore to suggest a method of forming the fossil shells he found. Furthermore, he refuted the idea that a single flood had been responsible for depositing fossils. As usual, da Vinci's views were centuries ahead of his time, but by the end of the 16th century the great Italian thinkers had established the organic origin of fossils beyond doubt.

The scientific study of fossils dates back to the beginning of the 19th century. William Smith (1769–1839), an engineer-surveyor, began to collect fossils as his work took him across England. A

1 Frontispiece of *Organic Remains of a former World*, Vol 1 (1804) by J Parkinson showing Noah's Ark in the distance with fossils washed up in the foreground.

surviving letter from Smith, written in 1796, comments on fossils and the regular distribution of particular types of fossil in characteristic rock types. He noted the 'wonderful order and regularity with which Nature has disposed of these singular productions and assigned to each class its particular stratum'. His recognition of a rock succession defined by fossils, and his resulting maps of geology, were the starting point of modern geological mapping and of biostratigraphy. Fossils played a vital role as Victorian geologists began to define the major geological periods.

The systematic collection of fossils, and their preservation in Museums, began in Britain around 1656 when a catalogue which included fossils was published by John Tradescant. During the Victorian period, museums were founded in all of the large British cities, many of which had collections of fossils at their centre. Despite funding problems over the past decades, British fossil collections remain some of the best in the world.

2 *Hyracotherium* is the earliest known horse from the late Palaeocene and early Eocene of North America and Europe.

Great collections 1: Natural History Museum

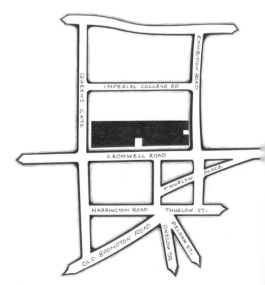

The Natural History Museum is the largest museum of its kind in the country. Purpose built to house collections of objects from the natural world, it has combined a tradition of excellence in display and research for 150 years. Its large and interactive displays on Dinosaurs and on the Origin of Man are outstanding. Working models of feeding dinosaurs and suspended reproductions of dinosaur skeletons thrill visitors.

The *Diplodocus* in the central hall of the Museum is surrounded by side cases of fossils, and the Waterhouse Way is lined with the marine reptiles collected by Mary Anning in the first half of the 19th century.

Most of the invertebrate fossils are displayed in the Earth Galleries. Fossils form part of a new interactive exhibition based on the history and evolution of the Earth.

Behind the scenes, the Natural History Museum has the largest British collection of fossils and fossil specialists, and is an international centre for research. Specimens will be identified by experts on request, and a full set of lectures and events is organised by the education department.

Natural History Museum, Cromwell Road, London, SW7 5BD. Tel: 0171 938 9123

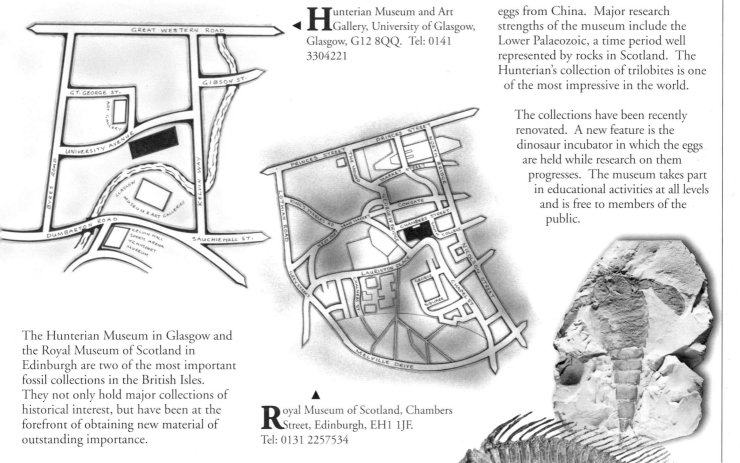

◄ **H**unterian Museum and Art Gallery, University of Glasgow, Glasgow, G12 8QQ. Tel: 0141 3304221

eggs from China. Major research strengths of the museum include the Lower Palaeozoic, a time period well represented by rocks in Scotland. The Hunterian's collection of trilobites is one of the most impressive in the world.

The collections have been recently renovated. A new feature is the dinosaur incubator in which the eggs are held while research on them progresses. The museum takes part in educational activities at all levels and is free to members of the public.

The Hunterian Museum in Glasgow and the Royal Museum of Scotland in Edinburgh are two of the most important fossil collections in the British Isles. They not only hold major collections of historical interest, but have been at the forefront of obtaining new material of outstanding importance.

The Royal Museum of Scotland holds and displays the rare tetrapod fossils from East Kirkton including Lizzie the Lizard (p.29). They also have pieces of Rhynie chert (p.30) and beautiful collections of Scottish fossil fish. Their latest aquisition is a perfectly preserved pterosaur from the Solnhofen Limestone which still shows its wing membranes (p.18).

▲
Royal Museum of Scotland, Chambers Street, Edinburgh, EH1 1JF. Tel: 0131 2257534

The Hunterian Museum is the oldest museum in Scotland, with collections made since 1770. It was opened to the public in 1807. Carboniferous sharks and other fish from Bearsden form a spectacular core to the Hunterian's fossil collection. It also holds a complete nest of dinosaur

53

Great collections 3: National Museum of Wales

An extensive, permanent exhibition on *The Evolution of Wales* was opened by the Queen in October 1993. These galleries show the geological and biological processes which have formed Wales over geological time. Fossils figure prominently in this exhibition, both as display objects and as carriers of information about the environment and climate of Wales in the past. In addition, the museum has a strong tradition for producing or showing temporary exhibitions of fossils including *Dinosaurs from China*, *Dinosaurs Alive* and *Mammoths and the Ice Age*.

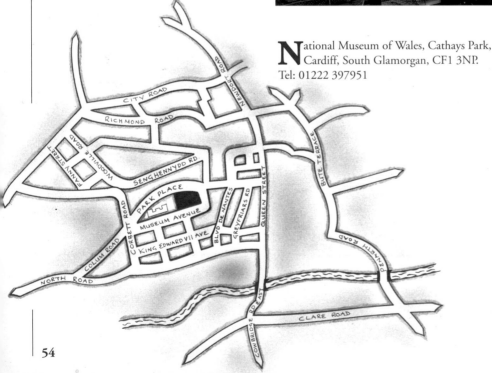

National Museum of Wales, Cathays Park, Cardiff, South Glamorgan, CF1 3NP. Tel: 01222 397951

The research collections at the museum are extensive and concentrate on Welsh fossils of all ages. Some of the earliest land plants are kept in the museum as well as important collections of Charboniferous plants. In addition, 30 icthyosaurs from southwest England, belonging to the Bath Royal Literary and Scientific Institute, are kept in the museum. Research is carried out at an international level, especially on Lower Palaeozoic fossils. Collaboration between the Museum and the University of Wales is highly developed, and the staff also work extensively with palaeontologists from overseas. The museum runs a full enquiry service for members of the public, and a series of walks is organised by the museum in various parts of Wales during the summer.

professor in Cambridge in 1818. It is out of his work that the Department of Earth Sciences, which is housed with the Museum, grew. Academics at the museum have always been at the forefront of palaeontological research. Their contributions have ranged from detailed taxonomy and biostratigraphy to major advances in our understanding of evolution. Over 9000 type specimens (that is, specimens which are held as the archetypal examples of a new species) are held in the museum. In addition, material from the Solnhofen Limestone and the Burgess Shale form part of the collections. Fossils have been donated to the museum by all of the great collectors and by many eminent scientists including Mary Anning, Charles Lyell, Roderick Impey Murchison and Charles Darwin.

Sedgwick Museum of Geology, Downing Street, Cambridge, CB2 3EQ.
Tel: 01223 333456

Over a million palaeontological specimens are held at the Sedgwick Museum in Cambridge, making it one of the country's largest regional repositories of fossils. Its core is a collection of rocks and fossils made by Dr John Woodward during the 17th century, the oldest intact collection in the world. More importantly, this museum has been a major centre of fossil research for over 150 years.

Adam Sedgwick was the leading geologist of his day and he became a

The Museum moved to its present site in 1904 and keeps a very Edwardian flavour to this day. The fossils on display are not only superb specimens, but are housed in the most beautiful teak and mahogany display cases. New displays include exhibits on Adam Sedgwick and a newly prepared icthyosaur. Activity days for children are held several times a year and the museum is free to visitors.

The major fossil groups

Trilobites

Dalmanites caudatus (1)
Taxonomy: Superphylum Arthropoda
Phylum Trilobita
Stratigraphic range: Cambrian to Permian
References in book: pages 8–11, 16–19, 24–27, 36–37

Trilobites were marine animals, inhabiting a wide range of ecological niches. Some were active swimmers, most crawled over the sea floor, while some were burrowers. They grew by a process of moulting, like modern crabs, to which they are distantly related. This means that each trilobite could leave several moults as potential fossils over the course of its life. Trilobites could see with a high degree of resolution through many-lensed eyes. The facial suture was a line on which the moulting skeleton came away from the body, leaving the eyes unharmed. Legs and gills were arrayed below the segmented body with two leg-gill pairs below each segment. These appendages had very thin and flexible skeletons and are very rare in the fossil record.

Brachiopods

Terebratula maxima (2)
Taxonomy: Phylum Brachiopoda
Class Articulata
Stratigraphic range: Cambrian to recent
References in book: pages 25–27

Brachiopods are twin-valved filter feeders, and are divided into those which have hinges between their valves (articulates) and those which do not (inarticulates). They generally attach themselves to the sediment with a fleshy stalk or pedicle. Brachiopods feed with a sticky ribbon, known as the lophophore. All articulate brachiopods sit at or very close to the sea floor. They were a dominant component of the Cambrian and Palaeozoic faunas, but they were supplanted from their dominant position in the Mesozoic. At this time bivalves, which are outwardly similar forms but with a much more flexible body plan, developed the ability to burrow and to filter from that position. This ousted brachiopods to a marginal niche in modern ecosystems.

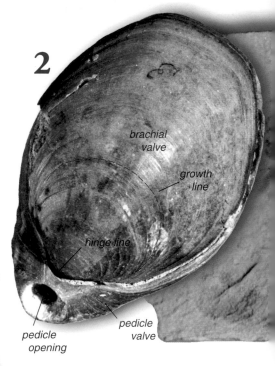

2

brachial valve

growth line

hinge line

pedicle opening

pedicle valve

1

segments

eye

glabella

facial suture

pygidium   thorax   cephalon

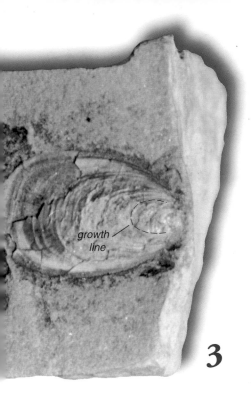

growth line

3

4

theca

stipe

sicula

lingulids are practically indistinguishable from modern forms.

Graptolites

Monograptus flemingi (4)
Taxonomy: Phylum Hemichordata,
Subphylum Pterobranchia
Class Graptolithina
Stratigraphic range: Cambrian to Permian
(planktic forms Ordovician to Devonian)
References in book: pages 2–3, 10–13, 16–17, 26–27

Graptolites were colonial animals which are all extinct, but they have living relatives in the modern pterobranchs, *Rhabdopleura* and *Cephalodiscus*. Graptolites evolved as bottom-dwelling filter feeders with a planktic larval stage. At the beginning of the Ordovician, this larval stage evolved the ability to mature in the water column and graptolites became planktic. They radiated very quickly in this new environment and rapidly took on new shapes. Ordovician graptolites had many stipes, accommodating up to 5000 animals in one colony. As time passed, simple forms with two stipes fused back-to-back became dominant. At the beginning of the Silurian period, single stiped graptolites appeared and quickly became the most common type. Rapid evolution and a widespread distribution have made them ideal fossils for use in dating the past. Comparison with their living relatives has shown that graptolites were well adapted to many different planktic niches, defined by the size and reliability of their food supply.

Lingula sp. (3)
Taxonomy: Phylum Brachiopoda
Class Inarticulata
Stratigraphic range: Cambrian to recent

Inarticulate brachiopods were most common in the Lower Palaeozoic but are still alive today. The best known genus is *Lingula*, a simple, paddle shaped form with a permanent gape from which the pedicle protrudes. *Lingula* is found today in shallow and intertidal environments and can tolerate wide fluctuations in salinity. Fossil forms occur in a greater variety of niches and it is possible that *Lingula* has been forced out of more highly contested ecospace with time. It is a perfect example of a living fossil: hard parts of Cambrian

The major fossil groups

Crinoids

Dialutocrinus milleri (5)
Taxonomy: Phylum Echinodermata
Subphylum Crinozoa
Class Crinoidea
Stratigraphic range: Cambrian to Recent.
References in book: pages 15, 26–27,
34–35

Crinoids, though animals, are commonly
known as sea lilies because they look like
flowering plants. Most are fixed to the sea
bed with a stalk and filter food from sea
water using a series of bony arms. They are
related to sea urchins and starfish and
share with them a characteristic five-fold
symmetry. They are common enough to
reach rock-forming
proportions at
some points in geological time, especially in
the lower Carboniferous. However, they are
rarely preserved intact as fossils. This is
because their skeleton is composed of a
series of small plates which are held together
by soft tissue. This decays rapidly after the
death of the animal and the plates fall apart.

arms

calyx

stem

5

Echinoids

Tylocidaris clavigera (6)
Taxonomy: Phylum Echinodermata
Subphylum Echinozoa
Class Echinoidea
Stratigraphic range: Ordovician to Recent
References in book: pages 4–5, 34–35

Echinoids, or sea urchins, are common on
modern shorelines and are part of the
hugely successful Mesozoic fauna. They
have five fold symmetry and are composed
of many small plates, in common with
crinoids which belong to the same
phylum. They are predators or
detritus feeders and have a well
developed jaw known as an
Aristotle's Lantern. They
move in an unusual
manner, on tube feet
which are filled with
water. The water is drawn
into the animal through the
madreporite plate and kept in
a series of valved regions which
make up the water vascular system.
Water is then pumped into and out of
the feet on demand. Early sea urchins
have true five-fold symmetry, but in the
Jurassic burrowing forms also developed
which have a secondary bilateral symmetry.

spines

6

hole for
Aristotle's
lantern

pores
for tube
feet

Corals

Isastrea conybeari (7)
Taxonomy: Phylum Cnidaria
Class Anthozoa
Subclass Zoantharia
Order Scleractinia
Stratigraphic range: Triassic to Recent
References in book: pages 14–15, 26–27,
36–39

All modern corals belong to this group of
scleractinian corals. These evolved
independently from the other groups of
corals from a soft bodied ancestor. Recent
corals are all marine and most live in
shallow, warm water with normal salinity.

Corals are usually colonial organisms and play a vital part in reef building, gradually adding skeletal calcium carbonate to the existing reef structure to develop an ever larger edifice. The Barrier Reef in Australia is a classic example of the size of structure which corals (amongst other groups) can build. Corals live in a symbiotic relationship with photosynthetic algae known as zooxanthellae. These live in the soft tissues of the coral polyp, which feeds from them. Some corals, although animals, have never been observed to feed from the surrounding water.

Palaeosmilia murchisoni (8)
Taxonomy: Phylum Cnidaria
Class Anthozoa
Subclass Zoantharia
Order Rugosa
Stratigraphic range: Cambrian to Permian

Halysites catenulaia (9)
Taxonomy: Phylum Cnidaria
Class Anthozoa
Subclass Zoantharia
Order Tabulata
Stratigraphic range: Cambrian to Permian

Tabulate and rugose corals were colonial reef builders of the Palaeozoic. They are similar to modern corals but arose independently from soft bodied groups of anthozoa. They were very common in Silurian and Carboniferous reefs of Britain

chains of individuals

9

and on a world-wide scale seem to have lived in equatorial latitudes in a similar distribution to modern forms. The shape of the coral colony was partly determined by the proximity of the individual corallites. Dispersed corallites had a round outline, but closely packed forms developed a polygonal shape. Tabulate corals are more simple than rugose corals and lack internal septae or dissepiments. The purpose of these structures was probably to allow the living soft tissue to make a snug fit on the top of the coral hard tissue. A few species of rugose corals, such as the example illustrated here, lived a solitary existence, rather than forming colonies. Some authors question whether tabulates were true corals at all. They suggest that the group might have been more closely related to sponges, which can also build a skeleton from calcium carbonate. The problem has yet to be fully resolved.

8

septa

dissepiments

columella

7

single corallite

septa

The major fossil groups

Ammonoids

Asteroceras obtusum (10)
Taxonomy: Phylum Mollusca
Class Cephalopoda
Subclass Ammonoidea
Stratigraphic range: Devonian to
Cretaceous
References in book: pages 2–6, 10–11,
16–19, 34–37, 46

Ammonoids were pelagic, or free
swimming, predators and scavengers
throughout the Upper Palaeozoic and
Mesozoic. They had a wide distribution
and evolved rapidly, so that for rocks of
Jurassic and Cretaceous age
they are of primary
importance for dating
rocks. There are three
main groups of
ammonoids which
form an evolutionary sequence. The
earliest are goniatites, which thrived in the
Carboniferous and Permian. They have a
very plain suture line made up of simple
plain curves. In the Triassic, ceratites
evolved, with a suture line half simple and
half crenulated. Finally the ammonites
proper evolved and flourished in the
Jurassic and Cretaceous. These are
characterised by suture lines of startling
intricacy.

Belemnites

Neohibolites minimus (11)
Taxonomy: Phylum Mollusca
Class Cephalopoda
Subclass Coleoidea
Stratigraphic range: Jurassic to Cretaceous
References in book: pages 34–37, 46

Belemnites are the internal skeletons of
octopus- or squid-like animals, which
would have been active predators in the
Mesozoic seas. The phragmocone
consists of gas- and liquid-filled
chambers, and the guard is made
from solid calcite. The combined
use of the two structures was in
regulating buoyancy like the cuttle
bone of modern cuttlefish. The soft
parts are rarely preserved, but in
the Solnhofen Limestone of Bavaria
traces of the belemnite body outline
can be seen. Also in this *lagerstätte*
are traces of a belemnite's probable
fate. Marine reptiles are preserved with
enormous numbers of belemnite guards
within their stomach cavity.

10

suture
line

umbilicus

venter

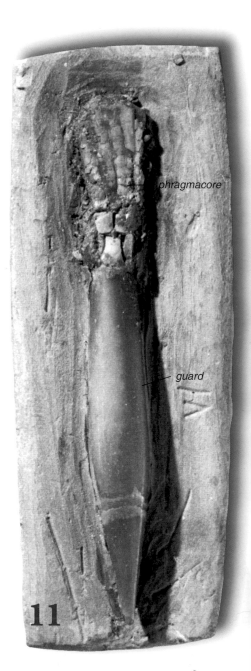

phragmacore

guard

11

Gastropods

Velutospinosa luetatrix (12)
Taxonomy: Phylum Mollusca
Class Gastropoda
Stratigraphic range: Cambrian to Recent
References in book: pages 26–29, 34–37

Gastropods or snails are among the most common molluscs and one of the few invertebrate groups to move into freshwater and onto land. Marine snails are most common in the fossil record and are present from Cambrian times. Gastropods became a significant component of the Mesozoic fauna which radiated after the end Permian extinction. They live in a wide variety of niches and are commonly scavengers or predators on other invertebrates. Some of the feeding habits of gastropods are memorably unpleasant: for example, some species have a very long breathing tube or siphon so that they can crawl into dead flesh but breath from aerated water drawn in from outside the carcass.

Bivalves

Venericardia planicosta (13)
Taxonomy: Phylum Mollusca
Class Bivalvia
Stratigraphic range: Cambrian to Recent.
References in book: pages 34–35, 38–39

On any beach the most common shells will be bivalves, a group which includes cockles, mussels, scallops and razor shells. Bivalves are molluscs, related to squid, octopus, ammonites, belemnites and snails. The phylum is one of the most diverse and successful on the planet. Bivalves evolved in the Precambrian and were amongst the first groups of organisms to form shells. However, they made up a minor component of the Cambrian and Palaeozoic faunas. Bivalves radiated dramatically early in the Mesozoic and form a vital part of the modern fauna. They are mainly filter feeders, but many groups live in burrows. This lifestyle protects the animal from predators or the environment and bivalves have developed many modifications of soft and hard parts to perfect it. Burrowing is achieved with a muscular foot, and water is drawn from the surface via siphons, straw shaped adaptations to the organism's body. Bivalves also use chemical and abrasive means to burrow into wood and into limestone. Some forms, such as oysters, can cement themselves together, another lifestyle which inhibits predation. Bivalves are tolerant of a range of conditions and species live in saline, brackish and fresh water. The life habits of fossil bivalves can frequently be inferred from features on the shell, making them very useful in analysing ancient environments.

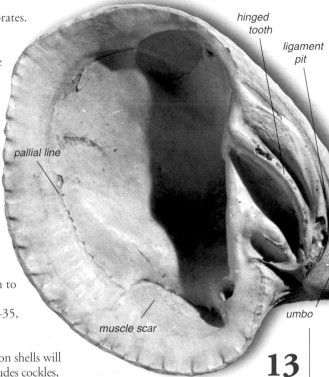

hinged tooth

ligament pit

pallial line

muscle scar

umbo

13

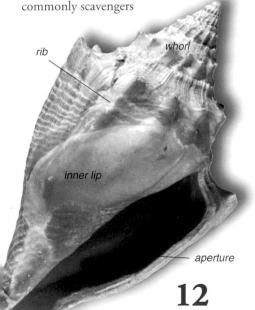

apex

whorl

rib

inner lip

aperture

12

siphonal canal

Index

Index

Acknowledgments, further reading & illustration sources

Acknowledgements

I would like to thank those members of the palaeontological community who lent me images for this book, or who corrected some of the mistakes I made in writing about their work. Remaining inaccuracies are, of course, my own. There are fewer errors of grammar and spelling than there would have been had my husband, Michael, not read the text several times. This book, as always, is dedicated to him.

Further reading

Invertebrate Palaeontology and Evolution by E N K Clarkson (1994). George Allen and Unwin. *The best textbook on the subject, dealing sequentially with all the common invertebrate groups.*

The Book of Life, S J Gould (editor)(1993). Hutchinson. *An excellent overview of the evolution of life.*

History of life by R Cowen (1995). Blackwell. *A detailed but accessible and extremely lively synthesis of modern palaeontology.*

Major events in the history of life, J W Schopf (editor) (1992). Jones and Bartlett. *Detailed, fascinating insight into the six events which the authors consider to be the most important steps in evolution.*

Palaeobiology: a synthesis, D E Briggs and P R Crowther (editors) (1990). Blackwell. *A series of short articles encompassing all the disciplines of modern palaeontology.*

Vertebrate palaeontology by M J Benton (1990).George Allen and Unwin. *A detailed introduction to the study of fossil vertebrates.*

Illustration sources

Front cover British Geological Survey (BGS)/National Museums of Scotland; Inside front cover BGS; 2.1 & 3.2 BGS; 3.3 BGS/Sedgwick Museum; 3.4 Richard Twitchett, Univ. of Leeds; 4.1 & 4.2 BGS; 4.3 BGS/National Museums of Scotland; 5.4 & 5.5l BGS; 5.5a BGS/Sedgwick Museum; 6,1 after Seilacher, 1985; 6.2 BGS/Sedgwick Museum; 6.3 BGS/National Museums of Scotland; 7.4 BGS/National Museums of Scotland; 7.5 BGS; 7.6 Simon Conway Morris, Univ. of Cambridge; 8.1 BGS source; 9.2 after Sheldon,1990, photos from the BGS; 10.1 BGS; 10.2 BGS/Segwick Museum; 11.3 after Mckerrow, 1980; 11.4 & 11.5 BGS; 12.1 Jane Francis, Univ. of Leeds; 12.2 BGS/National Museums of Scotland; 13.3 after Fortey and Cocks 1986; 14.3 BGS; 15.4 Jane Francis, Univ. of Leeds; 15.5 BGS; 16.1 Sören Jensen, *Lethaia*, Vol. 2, 29–42, Oslo; 16.2 BGS; 17.3 Martin Wells, Univ. of Cambridge; 18.4 BGS/National ___ of Scotland; 19.5 & 19.6 Richard Fortey, Natural History Museum; 22.1 after Schopf, 1992; 22.2 BGS; 23.3 & 23.4 Nick Butterfield, Univ. of Western Ontario; 23.5 BGS; 24.1 BGS/National Museums of Scotland; 25.2 Simon Conway Morris, Univ. of Cambridge; 25.3 BGS; 26.2 Sue Rigby; 26.3 & 27.4 & 27.5 BGS; 27.6 BGS/National Museums of Scotland; 28.1 after Edwards and Burgess, 1990 & Seldon, 1990; 29.2 BGS/National Museums of Scotland; 29.3 BGS; 29.4 BGS/National Museums of Scotland; 29.5 National Museums of Scotland; 30.1 Ed Jarzembowski, Maidstone Museum and Art Gallery; 30.2 & 31.3 Andrew Scott, Univ. of London; 31.4 Ed Jarzembowski, Maidstone Museum and Art Gallery; 30–31 background, Jane Francis; 32.1 Simon Conway Morris, Univ. of Cambridge; 32.2 BGS; 33.3 BGS/National Museum of Scotland; 33.4 & 33.5 Natural History Museum; 34–35 all BGS; 36.1 after Gould 1993; 36.2 BGS; 36.3 BGS/Sedgwick Museum; 37.4 BGS; 37.5 Natural History Museum; 38–39 all BGS; 40.1 after Susman, 1990; 41.2 Natural History Museum; 41.3 BGS; 42.1 BGS; 42.2 after Cowan 1994; 43.3 National Museum of Ireland; 43.4 BGS; 44.1 Jane Francis, Univ. of Leeds; 45.2 after Klein, 1982; 46.1 David Martill, Univ. of Portsmouth; 46.2 after Martill and others, 1994; 47.3 from an idea by Phil Stone (BGS); 48.1 Phil Donaghue/Richard Aldridge, Univ. of Leicester; 49.2 Paul Pearson, Univ. of Bristol; 49.3 after Anderson 1977; 50.1 BGS source; 51.2 Natural History Museum; 51 background, Sedgwick Museum; 52 Natural History Museum; 53 BGS/National Museums of Scotland; 54 National Museum of Wales; 55 Sedgwick Museum; 56–57 all BGS; 58–59 all BGS; 60–61 all BGS.

BGS Photography by Jim Evans and Tim Cullen.

This book follows the geological timescale of F Gradstein and J Ogg, *Episodes*, Vol. 19, Nos 1 & 2, 1996.